D1508114

KIEFER SUTHERLAND

Living Dangerously

Books by the Same Author

Dreaming Aloud: The Films of James Cameron (1998)

Ten Thousand Bullets: The Cinematic Journey of John Woo (1999)

Depp (2001)

Mickey Rourke: High and Low (2006)

Johnny Depp Photo Album (2009)

Christopher Heard

KIEFER SUTHERLAND
Living Dangerously

Published by Transit Publishing Inc.

ISBN: 978-1-926745-04-6

Editor: Timothy Niedermann
Copyeditor: Shannon Partridge
Proofreader: Nachammai Raman
Text design and composition: Nassim Bahloul
Cover design: Pierre Pommey and François Turgeon
Photos insert design: Nassim Bahloul

Cover photos:
© Sharkpixs/ZUMA/KEYSTONE Press
© Peter Foley/epa/Corbis

Transit Publishing Inc.
1996, St. Joseph Boulevard East
Montreal, QC
H2H 1E3

Tel: 1-514-273-0123
www.transitpublishing.com

Printed and Bound in Canada

Dedication

For Isabelle

Acknowledgments

First and foremost, heartfelt thanks must go to Ian Halperin. Ian has been something of an inspiration to me and was directly responsible for getting me involved in this book. Thank you, Ian.

Thanks also to the fine people at Transit Publishing, especially Pierre Turgeon and Gratia Ionescu. This has been the most enjoyable experience in publishing I have ever had. I am looking forward to the next one with you all as well.

Many thanks to Timothy Niedermann, my editor. His support, encouragement, and intuition helped this project enormously. I am very much looking forward to working with Timothy again on the next one.

Special thanks to John English, who was part of a brief but important time in Kiefer's life, for generously and graciously sharing his thoughts and stories with me.

Thanks to all the fine people at the Royal York, my home, from the general manager to the maids. You all made me very comfortable during this project.

Thanks to my family: my parents Marie and Bill, as well as my brother Peter. All have been completely supportive of everything I have chosen to do, even when those things were hard to understand.

Thanks to the beautiful Rhonda Thain, the wonderful woman who has lived this adventure with me; it has been much more exciting and rewarding because of her.

TABLE OF CONTENTS

PROLOGUE

I have to admit that the idea of writing Kiefer Sutherland's story was not an original one—it was suggested to me by my friend and fellow author, Ian Halperin. But I have been fascinated by the life and career of the star of *24* for a long time, so the notion took hold quickly.

I remember my first meeting with Sutherland very clearly. It was a sunny morning in September 1998, at the Four Seasons Hotel in Toronto. He was in town to screen his film *A Soldier's Sweetheart* at the Toronto International Film Festival, and I had arranged to meet him for an interview. Sutherland entered the room in dark gray pants and a crisp blue shirt with no tie. He moved with a slow, measured gait as if he were not just walking but ruminating deeply about something at the same time. He was slight, and while his receding hairline and angular facial features made him interesting to look at, his appearance was not what you would expect in a movie star. But once he spoke, his resonant voice—gruff but oddly soft and welcoming all at once—established his presence. This was a movie star all right. His handshake was firm and his demeanor friendly; he greeted the cameraman who was fixing his microphone with the same warmth and enthusiasm that he greeted me. Our conversation that day went well; when Kiefer Sutherland agrees to an interview, he comes ready and open to talk. I came away with the impression of a very serious actor: disciplined, hardworking, completely dedicated to his craft, and a thorough professional.

The next time I saw him was eight years later, again in Toronto. This time the setting was a restaurant in the chic section of town known as Yorkville. It was an evening in late June, and I was sitting with Mickey Rourke, the subject of a book I was working on at the time. Toward the end of our dinner, the quiet ambience of the restaurant was shattered when a roaring drunk suddenly jumped up on a table across the room. He pulled off his shirt and started waving it around over his head helicopter fashion, hollering at the top of his lungs about the unbearable heat and humidity. The drunk was Kiefer Sutherland. To say the least, this was a different man from the one I had met before. Or was it?

It is hard not to find Sutherland's life interesting: it is nothing if not mercurial. The son of well-known actors, he lived an unsettled early life. He nevertheless achieved serious fame at a young age as an actor in his own right. After his initial successes, his career became increasingly erratic, characterized by odd decisions, opportunities blown, and numerous personal and professional disappointments. Public drunkenness and outrageous and increasingly reckless behavior followed, culminating in a forty-eight-day jail stint in late 2007 and early 2008 for a DUI conviction and probation violations.

Through it all, though, there is one thing that sets Kiefer Sutherland apart from many of his mega-star colleagues. He is fully aware that his behavior sometimes lacks maturity, foresight, and logic. When called on his improprieties or lapses in judgment, he freely cops to them with a crooked, awkward smile and a declaration that, yes, he has acted like an asshole and is kind of embarrassed by it, and he will not deny that he did it, so why don't we all just move on.

The staggering success of *24* has not just breathed life into Sutherland's sagging career, it has catapulted him into a stratosphere all unto himself. His last *24* contract made him the highest-paid actor in the history of dramatic television—$40 million each for seasons Five through Eight. The name of his character, Jack Bauer, is now part of the common lexicon: a violent super-patriot who will use any means necessary to protect Americans from all who threaten them.

But while *24* has made Kiefer Sutherland the actor a global superstar, it is not clear it has been entirely positive for Kiefer Sutherland the human being. On-screen, his character relentlessly vanquishes terrorists who threaten America from without; off-screen, Sutherland is the one who is pursued—by demons that threaten from within. The worry is that the success of the series may have merely given Sutherland greater wherewithal to further his own self-destruction.

What I wish to accomplish with this book is give fans and interested readers a look past the plasticized gossip-column veneer that coats the lives of most stars and precludes the slightest glimpse of the real person underneath it. The function of any good biography is to put a human face on its subject, to make that person accessible. My aim is to gain insight into why Sutherland works as hard as he does and why he plays even harder. And while his personal behavior may be the main reason for his career difficulties, it is his astounding professional discipline that has allowed him to recover time and time again. He is proof that second (or third or even fourth) chances in life do happen if, despite the setbacks, you still believe in yourself and are able to be in a position to meet new opportunities head on. He has proved that redemption is possible, and in this way he can be an inspiration to others. But his story is also a cautionary tale, as it shows the sordid depths where self-indulgent, reckless behavior can lead.

The title of this book, *Kiefer Sutherland: Living Dangerously*, may say it all. In a way, it comes from Sutherland himself, from something he said to me during our first meeting on that September day in 1998: "My problem is that when I am not actually working or engaged in something that really interests me, I end up getting into trouble. If I don't keep myself busy I don't know what to do with myself, and I end up being where I shouldn't be and doing what I shouldn't be doing. It's a fucking dangerous way to live, man."

1

THE SEARCH FOR JACK BAUER

"I've made films that I've given all I had to but that no one has seen. The bottom line is I want to work and I want someone to enjoy it."

–Kiefer Sutherland

One morning in 2000, television producers Joel Surnow and Robert Cochran had breakfast at the International House of Pancakes in Woodland Hills, California, to discuss an idea for a new television series. The pair had had a surprise hit in 1997 with *La Femme Nikita*, which was not only doing well for the USA Network but had become an international success in syndication. Now, *La Femme Nikita* was heading into its last season, and they were thinking of another show along similar action-espionage lines. They wanted to use the format of a race against time to create dramatic tension, but with a twist: it would be in real time.

"I was standing in my house, between the shower and the sink, when the idea hit me," Surnow recalls. "I love numbers, adding them up, playing with them. Twenty-four hours in a day, twenty-four episodes of a show that would take place over a single day. That was where the idea began."

His partner Cochran's reaction was immediate and negative. "My head just hurts thinking about it," he told Surnow. "Don't ever mention it again." But Surnow called back the following day and over breakfast the two men hashed out how it would work. "We had to justify keeping the characters up for twenty-four hours. Full speed. On the edge," Cochran says.

What came out of that morning meal at the IHOP was a pitch for a new show that they called *24*. They wanted to take what they had done with *La Femme Nikita* several steps further, to push the boundaries of TV drama. The main character in *24* would be an agent with the secretive Los Angeles-based Counter Terrorism Unit (CTU). To humanize him, to get away from the lone-wolf stereotype that so many espionage dramas fall into, the agent would have a wife and teenage daughter. But to depict fully dimensional characters and maintain dramatic tension within a real-time format would be an extraordinary challenge. They would have to innovate, to develop new visual techniques to keep audiences connected to the various story lines.

Cochran and Surnow met with Fox TV's executive vice-president of programming, David Nevins, who was responsible for buying pilots and putting them into active development. Nevins was so taken by the pitch that he bought it on the spot. "Truthfully," Nevins says, "I hear hundreds of pitches a year and not often do I actually buy it in the room. But these guys came in and gave us something that moves the form of television forward. It was a bold idea."

"I was nervous going in because up to that point I had written eleven pilot scripts and none of them had been bought," says Surnow. "I was known as the gun for hire who comes in and runs a show, but this was the first thing I had created myself that actually sold, and sold quick. It was a good day."

Fox reportedly set a budget of around $4 million for the pilot. This is a high-end figure for a pilot and testifies to Fox's strong support for the project. Surnow and Cochran's small production company, Real Time Productions, didn't have the resources to give the pilot the production values that they knew were needed, so they approached Imagine Entertainment to be co-producer. Imagine Entertainment is owned by Oscar-winning film director Ron Howard and his partner Brian Grazer. Grazer initially had a bad reaction to Surnow. "I thought he was a loud-mouthed, obnoxious boor when I had that first meeting with them," Grazer says. "Then I got to really admire him and like him a lot. I realized he was just super-passionate about this project and was fully committed to it. Once I realized that, I knew that the project would be quite powerful; these guys would have it no other way."

Imagine Entertainment's involvement in the project had one early, unforeseen effect. In the original script, the lead character was named Jack Barrett. Gradually the producers came to feel that the name Barrett was too bland and started thinking of a replacement. There was an executive at Imagine named Ellen Bauer, and her surname fit. Jack Barrett was re-baptized Jack Bauer.

Surnow and Cochran set up for the pilot of *24* at Real Time Productions' studio in an old pencil factory in the San Fernando Valley. The ground floor of the building was converted into a soundstage where the sets for the main CTU Los Angeles offices were built and where a good percentage of the show's interiors would be filmed. Director-writer-executive producer Stephen Hopkins was brought in to oversee the creative thrust of the show. Hopkins agreed to executive-produce Season One and to write and direct at least half its episodes.

Hopkins had been working steadily in Hollywood since 1989, when he directed *A Nightmare on Elm Street 5: Dream Child*. He followed that with *Predator 2* and directed the big-budget film version of *Lost in Space*, among many other projects. Hopkins has the reputation of being driven and determined, operating with what might be called creative tunnel vision. He is intensely focused on achieving the exact artistic result he imagines in his mind, to the exclusion of anything he considers to be extraneous.

Surnow and Cochran admitted early on they had no real idea who would play Jack Bauer; they had never really considered any particular actor or type of actor when they were developing and pitching the idea for *24*. When the time came to cast the crucial roles of Jack Bauer, Teri Bauer, and Senator David Palmer, they set out to see as many people as they could in hopes of finding a good match for each character. But casting the lead role proved to be very difficult. "Even after thirty different actors, we really didn't have anyone who jumped out at us and said, 'Jack Bauer!' " recalls Surnow.

It was then that Hopkins suggested a name: Kiefer Sutherland. The others were understandably skeptical. This was not an A-list name. Sutherland had shown promise early on, but now all he was known for was a few 1980s-era Brat Pack movies. His career had trailed off in recent years into the purgatory of direct-to-video films, and, at the age of thirty-three, what little media excitement he generated came from his latest drunken exploits. Was this Jack Bauer? It didn't seem likely.

2

BRED IN THE BONE

"My parents not only did it for a living, they were really good at it."

–Kiefer Sutherland

Kiefer William Frederick Dempsey George Rufus Sutherland and his twin sister Rachel were born on the morning of December 21, 1966, at St. Mary's Hospital in the Paddington area of London, England. Their parents were a pair of Canadian actors, Donald Sutherland and Shirley Douglas. Both were pursuing their fledgling acting careers in London, where they had met and married a few months before.

In 1967, when the senior Sutherland's film career began to take off, they moved from London to Los Angeles. The marriage, unfortunately, lasted just four years. The couple separated in August 1969 and divorced in 1970. Sutherland stayed in the U.S., but Douglas, unable to obtain a work permit due to her past political activity, was eventually forced to return to Canada with the twins and her older son, Thomas, from a previous marriage. She settled with her children in Toronto, where she promptly set about restarting her career.

****

Since 1955, when she was cast in a couple of episodes of *Douglas Fairbanks Jr. Presents,* Shirley Douglas has been a prolific working actor. She was born April 2, 1934, in Weyburn, Saskatchewan, where her father was a Baptist minister. In 1935, when Shirley was just one, he ran for the Canadian parliament as a member of the Cooperative Commonwealth Federation. His election that year was the start of a career that made him a Canadian political legend. The CCF was a grassroots socialist party formed in Calgary, Alberta in 1932. It had a simple slogan: Humanity First. By 1942, Douglas had been elected the provincial leader of the CCF, and in 1944 he was elected premier of Saskatchewan for the first time, heading the first democratically elected socialist government in North America. He served as premier from 1944 through 1961.

Tommy Douglas is commonly remembered as the architect of Canada's socialized medical system while he was a member of parliament in the 1960s, but he contributed much more than that. For nearly twenty years, Douglas was an unstoppable force for positive political change in Saskatchewan. In his first term as premier, he paid off the provincial debt and balanced the books. He made sure that the provincial old-age pension plan included coverage for medical, dental, and hospitalization costs. He also left his mark on the provincial education system when he enlarged Saskatchewan schools and created a medical school for the University of Saskatchewan. On top of all that, he paved roads and provided electricity and sewer systems for areas of the province that had not known such things before. A very popular premier, he was re-elected four times and served for just over seventeen years. He returned to federal politics in 1961 as head of the National Democratic Party, the replacement for the CCF, which had disbanded that year.

As a child, Shirley Douglas sang and performed little plays on the stage of Cavalry Baptist Church, where her father was the pastor. The church is now the Signal Hill Theatre in Weyburn and is dedicated to the memory of Tommy Douglas. Shirley began her serious acting career when she was sixteen years old as part of the stage troupe known as the Regina Little Theatre. In 1950, the group entered the Dominion Drama Festival, an annual national drama competition held on Shakespeare's birthday, and Douglas won the prize for best actress. From there she dove head first into her acting career at the Banff School of Fine Arts, then in London, England, where she enrolled at the Royal Academy of Dramatic Art. She graduated after two years of study but remained in London to work in theater and film. Her first film role came in London in 1955 in the Shakespeare-turned-revisionist-gangster film *Joe Macbeth*. She returned to Canada briefly in 1957 but was soon back in England, where she continued to add to her acting credentials, including a supporting role in Stanley Kubrick's 1962 Academy Award-winning film *Lolita*.

In 1966, still in England, Douglas married fellow Canadian actor Donald Sutherland and delivered twins Kiefer and Rachel later that same year. The next year, however, the family moved to Corona, California, in support of Sutherland's suddenly burgeoning film career. While in Los Angeles, Douglas put her acting career on hold to care for her young children, although she was anything but a stay-at-home housewife. After all, this was Hollywood in the 1960s, and she had inherited her dad's bombastic, passionate dedication to causes she felt worth fighting for.

While she and her husband were both active in the protests against the Vietnam War, Douglas also joined the American civil rights movement alongside such heavyweights as Paul Newman, Marlon Brando, and Harry Belafonte. Shirley's passion for civil rights was so fervent that she helped organize a group called the Friends of the Black Panthers. The Black Panthers were ostensibly a black-power anti-defamation group that saw itself as a political party, but their black leather jackets, black berets, and ultramilitant rhetoric led the U.S. government and the FBI to classify them as an urban terrorist organization. A number of their members had major criminal records and were former street-gang members, and the Panthers had been linked to everything from bank robbery to murder.

In 1969, Douglas was arrested in Los Angeles on a charge of conspiracy to possess unregistered explosives. The LAPD and the FBI alleged that she had attempted to buy hand grenades for the Black Panthers to use in urban terrorist activities or bank or armored-car robberies to help fund their domestic revolutionary movement. Douglas herself believed that she was being framed as part of a very well-organized effort by various U.S. government law enforcement agencies to do away with the Black Panthers by any means necessary. The charges were later dropped, but after Douglas and Sutherland divorced, she was nevertheless denied a work permit on the basis of her arrest and was forced to return to Canada with her children.

Once settled in Toronto, Douglas got right back into acting. She played the title role as the famed feminist activist in the TV movie *Nellie McClung* and continued to work steadily in TV and film. Her passion for acting is unbounded. "It is a wonderful profession, full of tradition and history," she says. "But acting also allows you to gain a strange kind of immortality, and it allows you to become and experience what it is like to live the life of other people without actually leaving your own life behind. There is a wonderful power in that, don't you think?"

Douglas has continued to act regularly in Canadian films and TV shows and on the stage to the present. She has appeared in everything from films such as David Cronenberg's *Dead Ringers* to the TV shows *Corner Gas* and *Degrassi: The Next Generation,* and she played U.S. Secretary of State Madeleine Albright in the 2006 American miniseries *The Path to 9/11.*

Shirley Douglas's contribution to the arts and to theater in Canada has been richly and publicly rewarded. In 2001, she was awarded an honorary doctorate from Ryerson University in Toronto and gave a rousing and inspiring acceptance speech to an audience of attentive young film, theater, television, and new-media students. After delivering an astounding performance in the Canadian television movie *Shadow Lake,* she was awarded a Gemini (the Canadian version of the Emmy) for best featured actress. In 2003, she was made an officer of the Order of Canada, the nation's highest civilian honor; the same year, the arts community honored her again when she was awarded a star on Canada's Walk of Fame.

Douglas remains very active in political causes. Most recently, and fittingly, she has been on organizing committees, along with actress Sarah Polley and members of the band The Tragically Hip, to look at measures to strengthen nationalized health care. She has been the national spokesperson for the Canada Health Coalition and has also worked with groups such as the Toronto Health Coalition and the Friends of Medicare Toronto.

In 2000, Kiefer Sutherland had this to say about his mother: "She is such a grand person. I mean, she has a personal power about her. She is a commanding presence, which is what makes her such a good stage actor. Quite honestly, I am scared of my mother. It's not an unreasonable or paralyzing fear, but, simply, I am really afraid of her being mad at me. So whenever I do something that is somewhat lacking in good judgment, my first thought is always, 'Fuck man, what's my mother going to think?' "

* * * *

Kiefer Sutherland's twin, Rachel, shuns the limelight that illuminates her accomplished parents and brother. She also works in the arts, but in a very behind-the-scenes capacity. Bearing a striking resemblance to her brother Kiefer, she projects the same gentle softness, which is effortlessly built into her facial expressions and smile.

In 1991, when she was twenty-five, Rachel took a position as a casting assistant on the TV series *Beyond Reality*, starring Shari Belafonte, about some parapsychologists investigating the paranormal from their home base in a university lab. In 1997, when she helped out her brother Kiefer on a film he was directing called *Truth or Consequences, N.M.*, she became involved in a more hands-on way with the filmmaking process. On her brother's film she worked in the art department, in camera and electrical, as well as in costume and wardrobe.

Vincent Gallo, a co-star in the film, remembers the first time he saw her on-set. "I saw this woman working here and then there on different things on the set," says Gallo. "I kept noticing her because she looked just like Kiefer. Finally I asked Kiefer if he was related to her. He told me it was his much younger sister. It all added up, but then I wondered why she was working as a grip when her brother was the director. I cornered Kiefer on that too. He said it was because she wanted to learn about the process from the ground up. I had instant respect for Rachel from then on." And as for Rachel being Kiefer's "much younger sister," depending on which records you consult she is either seven or all of twelve minutes younger than her big brother.

After taking some time to learn the ropes, she joined the TV series *The Zack Files,* where she was post-production supervisor on twelve episodes. Most recently, Rachel has been post-production supervisor on two Canadian feature films: *You Might As Well Live,* starring Michael Madsen, and the highly regarded *Cairo Time,* starring Oscar nominee Patricia Clarkson.

Like Kiefer, Rachel had a wild early life—the international careers of her parents, the glare of the public eye, and the spirit of the times themselves were all contributing factors—and it certainly formed who she is today. But unlike her twin, she seems to have found some peace with herself.

* * * *

Donald McNichol Sutherland was born on July 17, 1935, in the city of Saint John in the Maritime province of New Brunswick, but he grew up in the small town of Bridgewater, Nova Scotia, where he graduated from high school. A performer and communicator at heart, his first professional job was a part-time position as a news correspondent for his local radio station, CKBW, when he was fourteen.

Upon graduation from high school, he headed to Ontario, where he enrolled at Victoria College, one of the seven residential colleges for arts and science students at the University of Toronto. The lanky, awkward Sutherland took to university life and began performing with the comedy troupe called the UC Follies. He was actually studying to be an engineer, with only a secondary major in drama. He graduated in 1958 with the double major, but quickly left engineering behind. It was while studying in Toronto that Donald met his first wife, Lois Hardwick, whom he married in 1959.

Sutherland headed to London, England, to pursue an acting career. Because Canada was a part of the British Commonwealth, Canadians and Britons could travel back and forth between the two countries and work or study with few restrictions. He enrolled at the London Academy of Music and Dramatic Art and immediately began trying out for small roles in film and television. He was first hired for a very small part in the anthology series *Studio 4*, in an episode called "Flight into Danger," and he continued to do small parts regularly from 1962 on. He snagged roles in a couple of the major horror movies of the day including 1964's *Castle of the Living Dead*, with the legendary Christopher Lee, and 1965's *Dr. Terror's House of Horrors*, which would become a cult classic.

Sutherland smiles when asked about this period in his life. "The thing about the British horror film—not just the ones I was in but the whole tradition—was that everyone took them very seriously. Everyone from the director of photography to the director to the actors was 100 percent into it, even though we all knew they were down-and-dirty, cheap horror movies. But because the audience could see us taking the stuff seriously, it became okay for them to take it seriously, which is why they are remembered as fondly as they are."

For Donald Sutherland, stardom arrived as a bit of a fluke. American director Robert Aldrich was in England casting a World War II film called *The Dirty Dozen*. In the film, twelve soldiers convicted of crimes and sentenced either to life in prison or death are asked to volunteer for a dangerous mission. If they succeed, they will all have their records wiped clean; if the mission fails, they will all likely die. Casting was proving to be difficult. John Wayne was

Aldrich's first choice as the main lead, Major Reisman, but Wayne was troubled by the vulgarity and the overt violence in the script. The role eventually went to Lee Marvin. Jack Palance wanted to do the film but insisted that the blatant racism of his character, Archer Maggott, be written out or at least toned down. The script stayed as it was, and Telly Savalas took that role. The film also starred the likes of Charles Bronson, John Cassavetes, Ernest Borgnine, and football legend Jim Brown.

The "Dozen" were divided into the "front six"—the stars—and the "back six"— lesser known actors filling what were essentially supporting roles. Just before filming was to start, however, one of the back six dropped out, and Sutherland approached Aldrich for an opportunity to audition. Despite the urgency of the situation, Aldrich was not initially receptive to Sutherland, not knowing him or having seen anything he had done. So Sutherland went to Roger Moore for help.

In 1965, Sutherland had been cast in an episode of the British television series *The Saint,* which starred a pre-James Bond Roger Moore. Sutherland made a good impression and was cast in another episode of the series late in 1966. That episode, entitled "Escape Route," was being directed by Roger Moore himself. "I remember Donald coming to me in a breathless state and asking if it might be possible for a film director and producer from America to see some footage of the show we had just shot," remembers Moore. He obliged and arranged for Aldrich to have a look at a rough cut of the episode of *The Saint* he had just directed. Immediately after seeing it, Aldrich cast Sutherland in the role of mentally slow killer Vernon Pinkley.

The Dirty Dozen proved to be a turning point for Donald Sutherland both personally and professionally. While the film was being shot, Sutherland divorced his first wife and married Shirley Douglas. Later that same year, just on the verge of his big break in American films, he also became the father of the twins Kiefer and Rachel. Knowing this was a propitious moment for his career, Sutherland moved his new family to Los Angeles. He found work immediately, appearing in one film after another for the next few years. None, however, brought him the audience or distinction that *The Dirty Dozen* had. Then in 1970 he appeared in two major films that would make him a bona fide star. Both were war movies, one set in Word War II, the other in the Korean War. But it was clear that both were antiwar films, allegories of the U.S.'s unpopular ongoing involvement in Vietnam.

The first of these movies was *Kelly's Heroes,* which also starred another young actor on the rise, Clint Eastwood, who had just come back from making his iconic series of "spaghetti westerns" in Italy. In *Kelly's Heroes,* a misfit group of soldiers is not only trying to bust through German lines but also to steal $16 million in gold bars from a German bank along the way. Sutherland was cast as a tank commander known as Oddball, with long hair, a full beard, and language like a spaced-out poet from Greenwich Village. While the film is set in World War II, Sutherland's look is very much that of a Vietnam-era hippie.

Then came the mega-hit *M*A*S*H,* in which Sutherland and his friend Elliot Gould co-starred as surgeons in a U.S. army field hospital during the height of the Korean War. Directed by the great Robert Altman, *M*A*S*H* became not just a popular film with big box office numbers and Oscar nominations but also a kind of cinematic touchstone for the era itself. Sutherland is very proud of the film. At the time he said, "This film has a real element of truth to it; it shows war without actually showing war. This is about the human damage and the psychological and emotional responses and resonating effects that war, a senseless endeavor, has on those involved in it."

Sutherland made several more films in the seventies, including the landmark *Klute,* in which he co-starred with Jane Fonda. He became romantically linked with the actress, even while still married to Shirley Douglas, as he and Fonda teamed up in protest against the Vietnam War. Subsequently Sutherland took on roles ranging from the infamous eighteenth century Italian adventurer Giacomo Casanova in *Fellini's Casanova* to a pot-smoking professor in *National Lampoon's Animal House* to the lead in the 1978 re-make of one of the greatest science fiction horror movies ever, *Invasion of the Body Snatchers.* One of his most striking performances of this period was as a cruel Italian fascist in the 1976 Bernardo Bertolucci epic *1900.* "My performance in *1900* is probably one of my best, but least favorite," Sutherland says. "When I first saw it, I was so disturbed by my character and my work that I don't think I have actually seen it again since."

In 1974, Sutherland met Francine Racette, his co-star in the Canadian film *Alien Thunder,* also known as *Dan Candy's Law.* They eventually married and had three children together: Roeg, Rossif, and Angus. Throughout this busy time in his career, Sutherland remained in touch with Kiefer and Rachel but was not particularly close to them, largely because of physical separation. Though Douglas remained in L.A. with the twins until 1977, Sutherland was often away for work. After Douglas returned to Canada, of course, the distance was only magnified.

In the early 1980s Sutherland continued to deliver the dynamism that audiences now expected from him. He starred in the Robert Redford-directed, multiple Oscar-winning *Ordinary People,* and in 1983 he starred in the Neil Simon-written comedy *Max Dugan Returns,* in which one of Donald Sutherland's fellow actors was a young, green actor named Kiefer Sutherland.

After starring in a couple of box office duds later in the decade, Sutherland turned in a powerful performance opposite acting giant Marlon Brando when the pair starred in 1989's anti-apartheid film, *A Dry White Season*. In the 1990s, Sutherland appeared in no fewer than thirty-nine films and TV shows. He settled into a comfortable niche as a supporting actor, delivering eccentric and unforgettable performances from his wonderful turn as an imprisoned pyromaniac in Ron Howard's *Backdraft* to his movie-stealing turn as Mister X in Oliver Stone's *JFK*. In 1995, he played Col. Mikhail Fetisov in the HBO thriller *Citizen X,* a film that earned him an Emmy Award as outstanding supporting actor in a miniseries or special.

The second time that Sutherland appeared in a film with his son Kiefer came in 1996, when both played small roles in *A Time to Kill,* an adaptation of the John Grisham novel of the same name. Their characters didn't have much interaction in the film, however.

As the new millennium dawned, Donald Sutherland was entering his fifth decade as a professional actor. He scaled back the volume of his workload, substituting some voice work for live-action roles, but he was still working steadily. He appeared in the Oscar-nominated *Cold Mountain* and the big-budget comedy *Fool's Gold* with Matthew McConaughey. Then he reunited with his old buddy from *Kelly's Heroes,* Clint Eastwood, in the hit film *Space Cowboys*.

In 2008, at the age of seventy-three, Sutherland was cast for the first time in a recurring role in a TV series called *Dirty Sexy Money,* a kind of adult soap opera set in the world of high finance. Sutherland plays the patriarchal character Patrick "Tripp" Darling III. With his flowing white hair and white beard and deep, resonant voice, the elder Sutherland is still a powerful presence, even on the small screen.

As the first decade of the twenty-first century draws to a close, Sutherland is still as active as ever. He lent his voice to the big-budget *Astro Boy* and has three other films shooting or ready for release before the end of 2010: *The Eastmans, The Love Child,* and *This Side of the Looking Glass.*

****

Interviewed in 1998, when Kiefer was at a low point in his career and had become infamous for his excesses off the set, Donald Sutherland reflected on the path his son had chosen. "I never encouraged Kiefer to become an actor, and I never discouraged him either. What I tried to do with Kiefer was to tell him, show him, what this is all about—all of it. Acting is one thing, show business is another. You have to be ready to face both." As for the public humiliation his son had gone through, "Having been through it myself, I know what that's like," he said. "But it is tough seeing your son go through it because there is a powerlessness that comes with it. I know what it's like, but I can do nothing to keep it from happening to him. All I can hope is that I have instilled in him the kind of strength of character that one needs to withstand it."

3

THE YOUNG ACTOR

"I'm not that complicated as an actor; I have a formula that I work with. I don't believe you can ever be someone else. You manifest different levels of your own personality to come up with a character."

–Kiefer Sutherland

Despite his parents' success on stage and in film, Kiefer Sutherland maintains he never really thought of becoming an actor when he was a kid. Through his early adolescence he did not know what he wanted to be; he just knew that his mother and father were so successful that he would not likely be able to live up to their achievements. But this began to change when he was in his early teens.

Interestingly, it was not his by-then-famous father who inspired the young Kiefer. While he knew his father was a movie actor, he had not seen a great deal of his work. "I had seen a couple of his films and loved them," he says, "but it wasn't until I was in my late teens that I really started to watch his movies on tape. It was with each viewing that my respect for him as an actor grew."

Instead, the spark that ignited Kiefer's passion for acting was seeing a stage performance by his mother when he was thirteen. It was in Ottawa at the National Arts Centre, and she was playing the part of Martha in Edward Albee's *Who's Afraid of Virginia Woolf?* "I don't think until that point I had ever seen my mother act in an entire piece," he relates. "But this particular performance just blew me away. As I was watching it, I stopped seeing my mother and was seeing only the character. Somewhere between the first and second act, someone I had known as my mother became someone else. The power of being able to do that both terrified me and moved me completely. I remember thinking that it would be a fantastic thing to do. I sat in the theater for a good twenty to thirty minutes after everybody had gone. I just kept staring at that stage," he says. "I slowly figured out that this void I knew nothing about—this gap between my mother and the character she played—was what was really cool about being an actor. And I wanted to learn about it."

As impressed as he was, however, it was another couple of years before he would reveal his desire to anyone else; when he did, it was, appropriately, to his mother.

* * * *

Years later, when Kiefer was thirty, mother and son would finally work together. In 1996, the pair took to the stage in Ottawa (and later Toronto) in the Shaw Festival's rendition of the Tennessee Williams play *The Glass Menagerie.* Shirley Douglas played Amanda, the mother, and Kiefer played her son Tom. "That was probably the most fantastic professional experience I have ever had," says Sutherland. "I was terrified going in, but I'm terrified about nearly everything. Then I realized that this is something I not only could do, but needed to do. I would be working with brilliant material, and I could make my mother proud and learn a hell of a lot from her at the same time."

Maclean's magazine reported on the pair's interaction on stage as follows: "At a quiet moment in the play, Amanda comes up behind Tom and comfortably rests her hands on his shoulders. Sutherland says the first time she did it, he realized that 'if someone else had done that to me, there would have been an initial uneasiness.' Douglas, watching her son, murmurs: 'Oh really?' Sutherland shakes his head: 'It was amazing.' A slow smile spreads across his face. 'I actually stepped out and acknowledged that I felt entirely at home.' "

* * * *

When Shirley Douglas returned to Toronto in 1977, she had very little money and the family lived very simply. "There was a time when we didn't have a couch, so we all sat around on the floor," remembers Kiefer. "We also were living for awhile in the first housing project Toronto ever had." Asked why his father, by now a Hollywood star, would let this happen, Kiefer shrugs, "Maybe he had offered my mother an absolute fortune. Maybe she didn't want it."

Douglas enrolled Kiefer and Rachel at the Crescent Town Elementary School in the area known as East York. After Kiefer completed grade five at Crescent Town, though, Douglas decided that he needed a more structured environment. He had developed a propensity for getting into mischief as a means of gaining attention, and often the minor incidents he was involved in would turn into something more serious. So, for grade six, his mother enrolled him at St. Andrew's College, an all-boys school located about forty minutes north of Toronto in the town of Aurora, Ontario. St. Andrew's is known for its discipline, and Shirley felt that this was something the young Kiefer was in need of. The St. Andrew's motto is "Quit ye like men, be strong," and the school declares its mission to be dedicated "to the development of the complete man, the well-rounded citizen." This sentiment, however, did not seem to resonate with Kiefer.

Although it was clear that he was intelligent, Kiefer was uninterested in school. He did not respond well to the structured regimen at St. Andrew's. The one thing Kiefer did seem to enjoy about it was sports. He excelled at track and field and was a good runner in his brief high-school career. Whatever he may have liked about it, the most significant thing he got out of his St. Andrew's education was a sort-lived nickname, "Reefer."

Years later, Kiefer would say that he had in fact liked the school. Five years after leaving St. Andrews he got back in touch with one of his teachers to sheepishly request a reading list from him. "I was seventeen at the time and dating a girl somewhat older than I was," he relates. "We were at a dinner one evening with a group of people, and I was horribly embarrassed when she was describing Truman Capote like he was her best friend. I asked her if that was one of her professors and was laughed at." From that point on Kiefer made it a point of reading everything he could get his hands on.

To try to get him more engaged with his school work, his mother transferred Kiefer to Toronto's Martingrove Collegiate Institute, a public school focused on advanced and gifted students. Douglas thought Kiefer might fit in better there because the school was designed as an open-concept environment, which was experimental at the time. The structure was loose, but the students were strongly encouraged to develop self-discipline with respect to their studies. The school has an intriguing Latin motto: *Lumen in vobis est*—the light is within you. Perhaps their particular brand of light wasn't within Kiefer, however, because he did not take to this school either. He neglected his academic work and started hanging out with friends, partying, and playing music. Music was becoming a passion of his. He had been exposed to music early, at five years old, when he began violin lessons. The violin didn't sustain his interest, but when he was twelve years old he began to play the guitar, which he kept up with avidly.

At Martingrove, he began to grow and fill out as an adolescent. This gave him more confidence in himself, though he didn't always apply it well. Toward the end of the school year, after he had turned thirteen, there was an incident when a classmate made fun of his sister, Rachel. Kiefer told the boy that if he did it again he would have to hurt him; then he turned and walked away. The boy charged after him and jumped on his back. To defend himself, Kiefer tossed the boy forward over his shoulder and attacked him. In the end, the boy suffered a broken cheekbone. "I remember that strange feeling," Sutherland says. "I was scared and panicked because I knew I had hurt this kid, and I knew I was probably going to be in some trouble for it. But at the same time I knew that I would be thought of much differently at school from then on in. And that was a kind of a powerful feeling."

Next stop on the Kiefer Sutherland school tour was Harbord Collegiate Institute. It is one of the older high schools in Toronto, first established in 1892. Alumni include the likes of filmmaker David Cronenberg, who grew up in nearby Little Italy, and former *60 Minutes* host Morley Safer. Located downtown, near the University of Toronto, Harbord Collegiate is a traditional school; its old cathedral-like building generally houses about a thousand students. It is also known as one of the most multicultural schools in the city.

Kiefer's time at Harbord was largely spent off-campus, however, in neighborhood cafés and social clubs; he enjoyed hanging out, drinking, and playing the cut-up with his inner-city pals. To keep him from falling in with what his mother viewed as an unsavory crowd, Kiefer was soon moved again. This time, it was Silverthorn Collegiate Institute, another old public school that was experimenting with a less rigid, more open-concept method of teaching. But Silverthorn, located in the residential Etobicoke area of greater Toronto, was not at all to Sutherland's liking. He quickly switched to Malvern Collegiate Institute, back in central Toronto, in the part of the city known as The Beaches. Malvern has been around since 1903 and also has a colorful list of alumni, from film director Norman Jewison to piano genius Glenn Gould to game-show host Alex Trebek. The school was renowned for its English program, and because Kiefer was now starting to show an interest in acting, it was thought that this was the place for him to be. Kiefer, of course, would only apply himself to his studies on his own terms—meaning whenever he felt like it—but he took to his drama and English courses, at least for a while. In his own mind he had pretty much decided that being an actor was not just something he *could* do but something he very much *wanted* to do.

Sutherland has his own take on his attitude toward high school: "It wasn't that I hated high school, even though it has to be one of the toughest, most socially awkward periods in anyone's life. It was just that most of my earlier life was spent traveling and being with show business parents who were always engaged and creative. To sit in a classroom and listen to someone drone on, it was almost impossible for me to connect with that."

In retrospect, acting seems like the most natural and understandable path he could have taken. But while the fact that his parents were actors obviously had some influence, most of his drive to act came from within himself. Kiefer struggled to gain acceptance from his high-school peers. He was nervous and awkward and tried to use humor to connect with other people. He tried to be the guy who made people laugh, the guy who everyone thought was wild and crazy, the guy everyone wanted to be around. And especially as he shuttled from school to school, he needed to know how to make friends quickly. He strategized how to be the center of attention, how to be entertaining. In short, he developed into a performer.

Kiefer had started taking drama lessons when he was just nine years old and had already made his acting debut at that age in Los Angeles, playing a small role in the play *Throne of Straw* at the Los Angeles Odyssey Theatre. The play, written by Harold and Edith Lieberman, has been described as one of the best pieces of drama written on the Holocaust. But it was only after seeing his mother on stage when he was thirteen that Kiefer's interest began to get serious. He began to attend acting classes on weekends, usually at Sir Frederick Banting Secondary School, in London, Ontario, over an hour away. "I started to really explore what acting was after seeing my mother perform," Sutherland remembers. "I thought it was just pretending to be other people, making believe, but watching my mother on stage showed me that there was a technique involved—a craft or an artistry. I was all of a sudden very interested in finding out how I could connect with those things. I wanted to know what an actor was, not just what an actor does."

By 1982, Kiefer, then fifteen, was done with school, at least in his own mind. A last attempt at Regina Mundi Catholic College in London, Ontario, ended with the same results. This was the last straw for his mother. She told her son that if he didn't apply himself, they might as well send him directly to jail, because that was where he was heading.

He began to talk of dropping out of school to pursue acting, but his parents were dead set against it. In the fall of 1982, they entered him in the Venta Preparatory School in Ottawa, but Kiefer knew he wasn't going to stay there; he was done. So one day, not far into his first term, he just left. He stayed with a girlfriend in Ottawa for a few days, then took a train to Toronto, where he intended to crash at the home of a friend named Greg.

He arrived at Toronto's Union Station at night. "I remember walking through that cavernous train station feeling excited, having butterflies in my stomach," said Kiefer Sutherland. "I think I had something like $46 in my pocket. I walked out of the station between these massive pillars. A small flock of pigeons took off in front of me. I remember thinking to myself that this is the first day of the rest of my life. I actually felt like Rocky when he climbed those stairs in the movie."

Because he was still only fifteen years old, he could not legally quit school in Canada. He thought he would stay hidden until December, when he turned sixteen and would be free to quit. But his conscience quickly got to him. He knew his parents would be frantic at not hearing from him, and, frightened of what his mother would do to him, he decided to call his father in California. He told his father that he was serious about acting and needed help to get auditions or an agent. Donald Sutherland offered to fly him out to the West Coast so they could discuss what was going on face to face. So, three weeks after he had left school, Kiefer was in Los Angeles.

His father was in the middle of making a movie at the time, *Max Dugan Returns,* a film written by Neil Simon and co-starring Jason Robards. Donald was able to get Kiefer a small role in the film to give the young man a little taste of what acting was really like. He did this on the condition that Kiefer re-enroll in school once the movie was done; he could pursue acting on the side, but he had to get an education. With this understanding, Donald sent Kiefer home to Toronto with a $400-a-month stipend. Kiefer was supposed to keep busy by studying and going on auditions. And indeed, he applied himself to these tasks, or at least one of them—acting. His mother helped get him his first agent, and he went to every audition the agent arranged for him. He was studying seriously, true to his word, but it was acting, not academics, and despite his promise to his dad, he put off re-enrolling in high school.

When Kiefer was making his run at being an actor, supported by his father, he lived in a one-room, lower-level apartment in an apartment house near Howland and Bloor streets in Toronto. "It wasn't even a one-bedroom apartment, it was just one room," he remembers. "The toilet was exposed and just concealed with a curtain. I would lay around in that little apartment listening to the Rush album *Hemispheres,* which I think I listened to for two straight years."

Kiefer was now on his own. Despite the continued support of his parents, he was living by himself and trying to make his own place in the world, on his own terms. To commemorate this new stage in his life, he decided to get a tattoo. "I was going to get Mickey Mouse in a space helmet. If I had done that [getting tattoos] it would have ended right then and there, but I ended up finding a Chinese symbol that meant something to me—it meant strength." He has continued to mark events in his life with tattoos, but this one may have been the most important.

Kiefer seemed to be finding direction in his life, but he was also showing an increasing pattern of reckless behavior, often fueled by alcohol and sometimes ending in violent confrontations. In 2004, he related to *Playboy* magazine an incident that occurred in downtown Toronto around this time. He was with his friend Greg. They had been drinking and decided to try to buy some weed from a dealer in a mall. "My friend looked at it and said it wasn't pot, it was catnip." They told the dealer that they wanted their money back. The dealer told them off, so Kiefer drew a switchblade he was carrying. He popped it open and told the dealer that he would stick him if he didn't give them their money back. "I never saw him punch me. Next thing I know I am waking up," Sutherland told *Playboy*. "I was knocked out, and my friend had been stabbed in the leg. The guy kicked the shit out of both of us, and I don't remember a single thing." The two returned home on the subway, Sutherland with his eye swollen shut and Greg with his leg wound bleeding profusely. At the end of it all Sutherland could only remember thinking, "I have got to learn to punch like that! That was good."

* * * *

There is a legendary theater in the area, the Bayview Playhouse, which was owned by the later award-winning documentary filmmaker Mark Terry. Terry himself staged both traditional and experimental plays there. A few were so successful that he ended up touring London and New York with them. "Kiefer's mother was a supporter of the theater and would often drop by to check out our plays," says Terry. "Kiefer would hang around as well, checking out plays; sometimes he would act in them. But he was really passionate about it, very dedicated and eager to learn."

The Bayview Playhouse was about to stage an experimental play called *American Modern*, by Peter Garrett. The sixteen-year-old Kiefer desperately wanted to play one of the leads, the very challenging role of a thirty-year-old man who is a mildly retarded homosexual. Although the character was much older than he was, Kiefer's passion and his commitment to doing everything it took convinced Terry to give him the part.

The first rehearsals of the play showed that it was very dialogue-heavy. Over two hours worth of dialogue had to be cut and that was just to keep the running time to an acceptable two hours. "The original writer of the play was fired," says Terry. "Kiefer soon learned the hard way that showbiz was not as glamorous as he may have thought, from life with his successful parents." Kiefer was so excited that he even asked his father to make the trip from Los Angeles to Toronto to see the opening. But as the opening drew nearer and nearer, the play was looking in ever rougher shape from one rehearsal to the next. Kiefer changed his mind. He called his father and told him not to come, as he didn't think the performance would show what he was capable of.

To roughen up his voice to be more convincing as a character nearly twice his age, Kiefer had doubled up on the number of cigarettes he was smoking. Then, just as the play was about to open, he came down with a terrible cold. It was suggested that the opening be delayed until he was in better health, but he insisted he could do it. "We decided to do help him out by quickly writing that his character had a bad cold into the script," says Terry.

The play opened and the newspapers that wrote about it—the *Toronto Star* and the *Globe and Mail*—were unimpressed by the piece. They found it too experimental, but both praised the young Kiefer for working beyond his level of experience and delivering a performance based on sheer guts and intuition.

Kiefer says of the experience, “This was the last long stretch of work [in theater] I had before I started working in film. It was a great experience for me; it taught me that acting, being an actor, was something I could do. I wasn’t afraid of it.”

There was no doubt that the Sutherland name and his mother’s connections in film and television in Canada would open doors for young Kiefer, but he still would have to earn his place on his own merits. “I never really considered that I would be handed things because of who my dad was or who my mom was,” he says. “You have to remember that when you grow up in a certain kind of life, that life becomes your normal; you don’t know what it is like to be outside of that existence looking in. So I never thought one way or the other about how I would get into acting. I knew that this was something a person could potentially make a good living at, and I wanted to give it a try.”

4

THE BAY BOY

"In a lot of ways I owe my career to Daniel Petrie. He not only gave me a great role when I had no experience at all, he instilled in me the confidence that I could think and act my way through a role at a very young age."

–Kiefer Sutherland

In 1983, after months of going to auditions, the now sixteen-year-old Kiefer got a reading with writer-director Daniel Petrie to play the male lead in the filmmaker's new project. The script was complex and thoughtful, and the lead was a role that just about every young actor in Canada was trying out for.

The late Daniel Petrie is not well known outside his native land despite his prolific film and television career. Petrie was born on November 26, 1920, and grew up in Glace Bay, Nova Scotia. He left Canada after university, and for the most part his professional career unfolded in the United States. Petrie's 1961 adaption of *A Raisin in the Sun* earned him the biggest praise of his career. At the Cannes Film Festival that year, the film was nominated for a Golden Palm and Petrie won the Gary Cooper

Award for Human Values. While he directed many other well-regarded films, including *Fort Apache, The Bronx* (1981), with Paul Newman, and *Cocoon: The Return* (1988), he never achieved the fame that his craftsmanship warranted.

For a number of years, Petrie tried to get a very personal film made—one that would be set in his hometown of Glace Bay, Nova Scotia, a former coal mining and fishing community on the north shore of Cape Breton Island. Once prosperous, Glace Bay's decline was all too evident when Petrie was a boy. But while there were certainly autobiographical elements in his screenplay, it was not primarily about his own life. Rather, Petrie wanted to capture the essence and the atmosphere of the place where he was born. He wanted to portray life in Maritime Canada with all its conflicting elements, where breathtaking natural beauty masks a punishing physical harshness. He called the film *The Bay Boy*.

The Bay Boy is the story of sixteen-year-old Donald Campbell growing up in Glace Bay, during the 1930s. Donald has had a strict Roman Catholic upbringing, and his mother is pushing him to remain in school and then enter a seminary to become a Catholic priest. But Donald likes girls and dreams of a life beyond Glace Bay. He has to deal with all kinds of dramas and upheavals, ranging from an attempted molestation at the hands of a priest to witnessing a murder committed by a local policeman who also happens to be the father of his sweetheart. There are many elements at play in this story: adolescent confusion, the harshness of life during the Great Depression and of life in a working-class Maritime town, where the weather and the remoteness bear down hard upon the lives of those who live there.

Made with the financial help of Telefilm Canada, the government film-funding agency, *The Bay Boy* had a small but adequate budget. It was produced by a couple of the heavy hitters in Canadian film production of the time, John Kemeny and Denis Heroux. While Petrie was happy to allow Kemeny, Heroux, and their executive producer, Susan Cavan, to handle the finances, he was concerned with the casting. Because the film was so personal to him, he wanted the casting to be perfect; he wanted each actor not just to look the part but to convey what that character meant in the overall tapestry of the story he was telling. His experience directing live television in New York in his early career had instilled in him the importance of good casting, of the careful matching of actor with character. But he had also been in Hollywood long enough to realize that making movies is a commercial enterprise and that he would need to have at least one actor with enough name recognition to ensure the film would receive good distribution. For *The Bay Boy*, the recognizable name belonged to twice-Oscar-nominated Swedish actress Liv Ullmann, the lead actress of choice of Swedish filmmaker Ingmar Bergman.

Kiefer's agent had arranged for him to audition for the lead role of Donald Campbell. Daniel Petrie of course knew who both Donald Sutherland and Shirley Douglas were, but he was not about to risk the lead in one of the most important films of his career on a young actor who couldn't pull it off, no matter who his parents were. So Petrie put Kiefer through his paces both in readings and on-camera auditions. This part was far from just handed to Kiefer—he had to earn it.

Years later, in 1999, the filmmaker remembered clearly that it was not Kiefer the actor he focused on; it was Kiefer the young man. "You know, it's funny, because I was looking for an actor to play that role who could portray a delicate combination of confusion and self-doubt but also determination and independence. Since I had nothing to judge Kiefer's acting on outside of his shaky reading and the material I put on video tape, I needed to rely on my initial instinct that Kiefer actually had that combination of qualities himself and was in fact going through his own not-all-that-dissimilar transition from youth to adulthood before he might actually be fully ready for it."

When the call came that he had been accepted for the part, Kiefer was still living in the apartment house near Howland and Bloor Streets in Toronto. "I was so excited when I got that job," he recalls. "I remember actually going outside in front of that little apartment and jumping up and down."

But Petrie then had second thoughts: "The kid [had] a haunting quality to him. He read for the part and won it. I had misgivings that night [though], thinking maybe there's just this wonderful dark side to him and he won't be able to play the comic lines. So I brought him back in and gave him all the funny lines, and he was delicious."

One of the other crucial roles in *The Bay Boy* was a young woman, Saxon Coldwell, the object of Donald's affections. Petrie's choice for this role, interestingly, was another young Canadian actor making her film debut and whose father who was also a renowned actor: Leah Pinsent, daughter of Gordon Pinsent.

Petrie decided to shoot primarily in Glace Bay, with additional filming in Sydney, about ten miles away. Sutherland joined the rest of the cast and crew at the local Holiday Inn where they were being housed. Upon checking in and going to his room, he closed the door and allowed the new sensation of being a working actor in an actual film to wash over him. "It was a great feeling. I remember catching my reflection in a glass door and smiling to myself and thinking, 'I did it. Here I am. This must be what I was meant to do.' "

His feeling of having arrived was shaken just a few hours later when the cast and crew assembled at a nearby Chinese restaurant for a dinner together. After dinner, Kiefer cracked open his fortune cookie to find a slip of paper that read, "Go Home." Despite the personal challenges for Kiefer, the filming of *The Bay Boy* proceeded uneventfully under Petrie's skillful hand.

"Kiefer was trying hard, and his instincts were all very good," Petrie said of his young lead. "So it was my job to direct those instincts where I needed them applied. But Kiefer was also filled with fears: fear of disappointing me, fear of disappointing his parents. If I couldn't help him get over those fears, the performance would not have been there."

For his part, Sutherland is nothing but grateful to Daniel Petrie for the opportunity he gave him and the faith he showed in him—the care he took to bolster the young actor's confidence. "I remember one day on the set I was talking to the camera crew," Sutherland says. "They were all Quebecois, and, man, those guys had style. I was trying to position myself to get a job with them as a runner or something in case the acting thing didn't work out. I was being self-effacing, putting myself down, when I felt a tap on my shoulder. I turned around and there was Dan. He quietly pulled me aside and then quite sternly said, 'You are simply not allowed to talk that way on my set.' He looked me straight in the eye and said, 'I am not going to let you fail here because that is my job. And as your friend I am not going to let you quit just because you're scared.' " That was precisely the kind of guidance Kiefer Sutherland needed at that moment.

Sutherland's performance is wonderful in the film. It is measured and thoughtful and captures the awkwardness and confusion of his character perfectly. For his part, Daniel Petrie does a magnificent job of telling a complicated story in a simple way. The landscape and local scenery capture the childhood vistas that he wants us to remember with him. He also directed the film's seduction scenes with taste and wonderful visual style. *The Bay Boy* is a great example of how good an English Canadian movie can be when everyone involved is committed to telling a good Canadian story.

The Bay Boy was unveiled to acclaim on September 6, 1984, at the Toronto International Film Festival. Later, Petrie arranged for a special premiere to be held in Glace Bay to thank the town for embracing the production. *The Bay Boy* went on to be nominated for eleven Genie Awards in 1985, the Canadian equivalent of the Academy Awards. Kiefer Sutherland was nominated for best performance by an actor in a leading role, and Leah Pinsent was nominated in the category of best supporting actress. In the end, *The Bay Boy* won six Genies that year, including best picture. Daniel Petrie won for his screenplay, and Alan Scharfe was awarded best supporting actor. The film also took the top honors for art direction, costume design, and sound editing.

Personally, director Daniel Petrie was also pleased. It had been a labor of love from the start, and he had spent years thinking about it and then writing it. "You know, it actually turned out better than I thought. I wanted to capture a mood and a drama that I remembered from my youth, and the film itself goes beyond that. It captured the moods and dramas of not just me, but a lot of the people I knew then. I also have a deep feeling—I am not sure what it is—for Kiefer Sutherland. He was able to be the Bay Boy I needed him to be."

Sutherland remains sincerely appreciative of the chance Petrie gave him. "There are lots and lots of great actors out there. What makes the difference between one actor shining or gaining a certain kind of popularity over another is simply opportunity—getting an opportunity and doing the right thing with it whether you are aware you are doing the right thing or not. *The Bay Boy* was my opportunity."

Daniel Petrie died in 2004 in Los Angeles and was given a posthumous lifetime achievement award from the Directors Guild of Canada a year later. Kiefer Sutherland presented the family with the award. Kiefer wrote his speech himself and delivered it with a sincerity that caused him to well up with emotion a number of times as he spoke. "Dan gave me my opportunity. Not only did he do that, he showed me a standard of quality and excellence in production that I still use as a measuring stick today. It would start with how graciously he treated and inspired his cast and crew. There was a nurturing quality to Dan like that of an all-knowing father."

Kiefer took the confidence Daniel Petrie's fatherly inspiration gave him and ran with it. His first stop was New York City.

THE ROAD TO HOLLYWOOD

"After I finished The Bay Boy *I had about thirty grand in my pocket. I thought that was all the money in the world. So me and my girlfriend and a couple of pals decided to roll the dice and head to New York City."*

–Kiefer Sutherland

In September 2008, it was reported that Kiefer Sutherland had just completed a deal to purchase a home in New York City: a five-storey Greek Revival townhouse in the West Village, built in the 1830s, with five bedrooms and an elevator. The price tag was a whopping $8.2 million. But due to a maneuver only Jack Bauer's alter ego could pull off, that price was several million less than the home was originally selling for. First listed at nearly $13 million, the price was lowered to $10.4 million, and when there were no takers at that price, it was lowered again to $9.4 million. Sutherland, under the guise of a cleverly created trust, came in and said he was interested, but another $1.2 million had to be shaved off or there would be no deal. He got his deal.

* * * *

When Sutherland first hit New York City in 1985, it was under rather different circumstances. The eighteen-year-old had come to New York with friends, full of a confidence that was new to him. His experience on *The Bay Boy* had been exhilarating—reaction to the film and his role in it were extremely positive. He felt that his show-biz name coupled with the award-winning feature film he had under his belt were what he needed to succeed as an up-and-coming actor in New York. He was right, but only up to a point.

"I thought I could retire on that money, man," he says now. "And it was enough to get a good jump on things. I was able to pay the tuition fees for my girlfriend to get into the Circle in the Square Theatre School, which was something she really wanted." The Circle in the Square is right in the heart of New York's theater district and offers actors the opportunity to train with working Broadway professionals. Kiefer's money also meant they could afford an apartment in the city for about a year.

In the end, New York was little more than a temporary stopping point for Sutherland before he headed toward Hollywood. Still, and despite his youth, he was forming habits that would stick with him through adulthood. Not all of these were good habits, however. Looking back on that period in his life, Sutherland describes the differences between New York and L.A. "New York is a vibrant place where, if you're looking for trouble, you can always find it," he says. "But Los Angeles, that's a place where you just stand still and trouble finds you." These were prophetic words.

It was in New York during this time that he had another brush with marijuana. He told *Playboy* magazine about a hilarious episode during this period that convinced him grass was not his scene:

"My girlfriend at the time said that pot was good for sex, so I went running down to Central Park and picked up a dime bag. We smoked it while watching TV. We started kissing and making love. I got really stoned, and my mind started drifting off somewhere else, thinking about what I had to do the next day, wondering what my parents were doing, where my sister was. I thought about everything but sex. I was moving very quickly. I remember specifically that when we started kissing there was a very funny car salesman on the television riding on an elephant. When we ended I felt great. I thought my girlfriend was right: this was fantastic. I rolled over, and the car salesman was waving good-bye. All of this had taken place in the span of a two-minute commercial. I said, 'Okay, that's it. Pot is not for me.' "

While in New York, Sutherland read and studied and played music while meeting with agents and going to casting calls. In one case he read for a role on a soap opera, even though he wasn't sure whether that was work he wanted to do or even could do. Soap-opera actors are worked famously hard and memorize pages and pages of script virtually overnight, day in and day out. When Kiefer was subsequently called and asked if he was interested in the role, he told the producers that he would think it over and get back to them. He then went to an agent and said he would turn down the soap-opera role and the $100,000 a year that came with it if the agent would take Kiefer on as a client and seek out movie roles for him. The agent was impressed by the young actor's drive and focus and promptly signed him.

Months went by with more auditions and more readings, but no work. The money from *The Bay Boy* was carrying him through, but it was beginning to dwindle. With no jobs in sight, Kiefer began thinking about heading west to Los Angeles to give Hollywood a try.

Finally, he auditioned for a print ad for Levi's and got it. "I was going out for anything at that point. If it meant a paycheck I was interested in giving it a shot."

With the few thousand dollars that Sutherland earned for doing the print ad, he bought a used car and put $2,700 into a cashier's check for him and his girlfriend to use as a stake when they arrived in California. They affectionately named their car, a 1969 Mustang, Lucy. Their journey began with high hopes, but before they even arrived in L.A. Kiefer's girlfriend realized that she had lost the cashier's check. It was all they had to tide them over once they got to Los Angeles until one of them secured work. "That was a real blow," says Sutherland. "But it was still an adventure, and it was what it was—the money was gone. When we arrived in L.A., we had no money, and that was simply the spot we were in." His father might have helped, but Kiefer didn't ask him. "The only way he would have known I had headed to L.A. was if I picked up the phone and called him to tell him, and I didn't want to do that." So Kiefer and his girlfriend were effectively on their own. Flat broke, the couple was forced to park at the beach, live in their car, and make use of public showers.

They had been living like bums on the beach in their 1969 Mustang named Lucy for about three weeks when Kiefer got an audition with Steven Spielberg.

* * * *

By the time Kiefer and his girlfriend landed on the beach in L.A., filmmaker Steven Spielberg had been the reigning king of Hollywood for a decade. Spielberg's 1975 film *Jaws* had redefined the summer blockbuster, as would 1981's *Raiders of the Lost Ark* and

1982's *E.T.* Now, in the mid-1980s, Spielberg was in a position to do anything he put his mind to. He had been toying with the idea of recreating the kind of anthology series that inspired him as a kid—a program like *The Twilight Zone* or *The Outer Limits,* based on the pulp adventure magazines that were very popular in the 1930s, '40s, and '50s. He had successfully re-established aspects of the formula with *Raiders of the Lost Ark* and the other Indiana Jones movies, but he felt that television would be the place to take the concept back to the grassroots level that had inspired him. With this in mind, he created *Amazing Stories,* named after the venerable science-fiction magazine Spielberg had read as a child.

The series had a great deal of promise, not the least because Spielberg committed to direct episodes and to write or co-write many of the teleplays as well. *Amazing Stories* debuted on NBC on September 29, 1985, with a haunting episode called "Ghost Train," about an old man waiting to board a train that he believes he caused to derail and crash in his youth. The tracks are gone, but the old man believes the train will return for him and take him away to his death. Spielberg directed the episode, which featured, among others, the young actor Lukas Haas, fresh from starring in *Witness* with Harrison Ford.

Spielberg was known for his ability to spot young talent and was using this series as a training camp of sorts for developing young actors and writers. Spielberg said at the time, "Because these [*Amazing Stories* episodes] are short-form pieces, and because it is an ongoing series, there is less pressure on the young actor to carry [the story than on] a big motion picture, so they can be more relaxed and more demonstrative in terms of showing us what they have."

* * * *

Sutherland looked forward to his shot with Hollywood's top director with trepidation. "I remember getting the meeting with Steven Spielberg and being anxious and excited at the same time," he recalls. "I was in awe that I was living in a fucking car on the beach but going in to meet Steven Spielberg. There was something magically surreal about it. So I went in and gave him my best."

He got the part. Whether it was attributable to his brilliance, good timing, or simply blind luck, the first job that Kiefer Sutherland got on his own merits in Hollywood came from none other than Steven Spielberg. (His first actual role had been two years before, when Donald Sutherland had secured a small part for Kiefer in *Max Dugan Returns*). Sutherland's role was in the fifth episode of the first season of *Amazing Stories,* entitled "The Mission." It was later considered to be one of the most special pieces in the two-year run of the series, principally because it was the only episode to run sixty minutes rather that the thirty-minute norm. The story concerned the crew of a B-17 bomber returning from a World War II bombing run. The belly gunner is trapped in his turret, and the plane's landing gear has malfunctioned. If they try to do a crash landing, he will certainly be crushed under the body of the plane. But the gunner, an aspiring cartoonist, is able to use his wildly infectious imagination to save them.

Sutherland played the role of Static, the crew's radio operator. Kevin Costner played the captain. This would be Costner's last time on television for a long while; his breakthrough movie, *Silverado,* was released the same year, catapulting his career into mega-stardom. Kiefer held his own with the other young actors, among whom were Casey Siemaszko, who would later co-star with Sutherland in *Stand by Me* and *Young Guns,* and Anthony LaPaglia, later of TV's *Without a Trace,* in a small role as a mechanic. LaPaglia later recalled the experience. "I was just so happy to be in the show, to be directed by Steven Spielberg. I knew Kiefer was doing his first gig. Costner was pretty much the guy to watch because of *Silverado,* but he was still trying to make his name. It was a magical show, both the show itself and what it meant for a lot of us."

The episode first aired on November 3, 1985, and Sutherland's career was off and running.

* * * *

Predictably, Sutherland found that having the name Spielberg on your résumé not only gets you meetings, it gets you jobs. So naturally, he used it as often as he could in the subsequent weeks as he searched for more work. And it bore fruit, which Sutherland readily acknowledges: "After that early role in 'The Mission' for Spielberg, I really never stopped working unless I chose to."

* * * *

Sutherland's next role was every bit as magical as this first experience with Spielberg, but for different reasons. *At Close Range* may be one of the most underrated American films of the last thirty years. The film was not seen by the audience it deserved, largely because of distribution problems. But to many critics it is one of the great American films in recent memory. The story is loosely based on the true story of a Pennsylvania criminal who involved his own sons in his gang. In the screenplay, which closely parallels the actual events, one of the sons turns informant after the father rapes his girlfriend. When the authorities begin to question gang members, the father plots to have all of them killed, including his sons. The oldest son survives the attack and testifies against his father at his trial.

The screenplay was written by accomplished writer Nicholas Kazan (son of renowned director Elia Kazan) but had languished for years, despite *American Film* magazine's description of it as one of the best unproduced American screenplays ever. Finally the script was picked up, and James Foley, a promising filmmaker, was chosen to direct. Robert DeNiro was originally offered the role of the father, Brad Whitewood Sr., but turned it down because he thought the subject matter too dark. The role fell to Christopher Walken, who took it and delivered one of his most chilling performances ever.

Sean Penn, who was in the news at the time for his turbulent marriage to pop singer Madonna, played the role of Brad Whitewood Jr. with a searing brilliance. Penn also worked closely with director James Foley on the producing of the film as well, and Sutherland always credits Penn with giving him the role of Tim, a friend of the Whitewood boys. In the finished film, unfortunately, Sutherland appears in only a couple of scenes; the bulk of his performance was cut out. Director James Foley explained this, saying, "Kiefer's role was bigger in the script and in the earlier cuts of the film. But this film needed to be very tight in order to work, so a lot of the supporting characters were cut down to keep the focus on Brad Sr. and Brad Jr. But when Kiefer was cast, he was cast as a good young actor, not just as a kid to stand around."

For Sutherland it was the second opportunity in a row to work with someone he deeply admired. "The reason that I came down to the States to try to get in films here was largely because of the influence of Sean Penn," he says. "When Sean and Timothy Hutton and Tom Cruise did *Taps* it really turned me on to what young actors could do, and it was that film and other things that Penn was doing that opened the floodgates for a lot of young actors to be taken seriously." He told interviewer Lawrence Grobel that he stayed close to Penn on the Tennessee set: "When we did *At Close Range,* normally we would chat beforehand, but I noticed that he was really quiet one day. I asked him later about it, and he said he always used to be excited on the set, hanging out and talking with everybody, but by the time he did his scene he had no energy. He learned that on specific days he should stay to himself so every ounce of energy he had would be put into the work. I thought that was smart, and I learned a lot from it."

* * * *

Kiefer's fourth film, and third high-profile acting job in a row, finally gave him the Hollywood acceptance that hundreds of young actors strive for. Within the span of a few short months, he had gone from sleeping in his car on the beach to filming in the desert with Steven Spielberg to shooting on location in Tennessee with Sean Penn. But now he stepped up to a higher rung on the ladder of Hollywood stardom. This fourth film was Rob Reiner's *Stand by Me.*

Like *The Bay Boy, Stand by Me* is a tale of youth remembered and youth endured, based on Stephen King's novella *The Body*. As happens so often in Hollywood, this project had endured a long and complicated gestation period. Originally the film was to have been directed by Adrian Lyne, but he was tied up with another complicated movie he was making at the time, *Nine and a Half Weeks*. Columbia Pictures had a firm start date for *Stand by Me,* so the decision was made to replace Lyne with Rob Reiner. For the role of the writer, the adult who tells the story in flashback, Reiner first cast character actor David Dukes but afterward decided the match wasn't right. He then considered his *Spinal Tap* star Michael McKean before finally settling on his old friend Richard Dreyfuss.

Stand by Me features a wonderful cast of young actors in the early stages of their careers: River Phoenix, who later died tragically of a drug overdose at the age of twenty-three; Jerry O'Connell; Corey Feldman; Wil Wheaton; and Casey Siemaszko. The film tells the story of a writer named Gordie LaChance who, after the death of a friend, reflects upon his life and one particular incident that shaped it. The film then flashes back to LaChance and his friends as young teenagers. Hearing that the body of a boy who has been killed by a train is lying next to some tracks across town, they set off to find the body and maybe get a little notoriety by reporting it to the authorities. In the course of their adventure, the boys learn lessons from one another about the value of friendship, understanding, and forgiveness.

One of the coveted roles in the film was that of a tough guy, the town bully, named Ace Merrill. Kiefer Sutherland auditioned for the role and greatly impressed Reiner. "Remember, *Stand by Me* was just my third film as a director," Reiner says. "So while I was confident, I was still anxious about the kind of crucial casting mistakes that can make all the difference in the world for your film. With Kiefer I had no doubt at all that he was going to be great as Ace. I remember him telling me that he was going to be the biggest asshole in the world, so much so that I would probably fire him from the film so I wouldn't have to be around such an asshole. He gave his role not just the depth I needed, but he made it his own by taking it in a few directions that I didn't think of."

As shooting progressed, Sutherland gained full possession of the confidence he needed to be a real movie star. He devoured his Ace Merrill role and stayed in character throughout the shooting, so much so that he would actually pick on Wil Wheaton and Corey Feldman off the set as well as on. One day River Phoenix decided to push back and covered Sutherland's car with a thick layer of mud. "When I found out that River had done that," said Sutherland, "I chased him down and treated him just as Ace Merrill would have treated him."

Co-star Jerry O'Connell puts it this way: "I wasn't scared of anybody on the set. I was a kid from New York coming out to Hollywood; nobody scared me. Kiefer Sutherland scared me! He really made himself very menacing to the four of us. Looking back, he was doing it just to be in character, to make sure we were scared of him. And man it worked! I was scared of that dude."

Stand by Me was a late-summer release in 1986 and went on to capture the hearts—and box office dollars—of a very wide audience. Stephen King himself has said that he thought it was one of the best adaptations of his work ever brought to the screen. Screenwriters Raynold Gideon and Bruce Evans were nominated for an Oscar for best adapted screenplay, and everyone involved earned overwhelmingly positive reviews. For Kiefer Sutherland this was yet another rung up the ladder.

Sutherland was making lots of money, getting attention, working constantly, and starting to get a real taste of what being a movie star was like. He was at a dangerous age to have that happen, and inevitably he started experimenting with drugs, particularly cocaine. While he is open about having used it, even excessively, he has made it clear that it wasn't for him. He told interviewer Lawrence Grobel, "I did it (cocaine) for a year, loved it, then just stopped." And while he used marijuana as well, he also decided early on that it wasn't really something he wanted to keep doing.

For his next projects, Sutherland did a pair of quick made-for-television movies, *Trapped in Silence* and *Brotherhood of Justice.* In *Trapped in Silence,* Sutherland was presented with a challenging role, that of a young man was being studied by a team of psychologists because he simply refuses to speak, although there is nothing physically wrong with him. Sutherland's performance in the film is both sensitive and technically brilliant.

Brotherhood of Justice, on the other hand, was a cliché-ridden film about a group of young vigilantes. Sutherland's co-stars included fellow Canadian Keanu Reeves and Billy Zane, who became a close friend. At the time, Zane was sharing the coach house of what was Charlie Chaplin's old mansion with Robert Downey Jr. and his girlfriend at the time, Sarah Jessica Parker. After they finished shooting, Kiefer hung out with Zane at the house and got to know everyone there. And since there was an extra bedroom, Kiefer was eventually asked if he would like to move in. At the time, Robert Downey Jr. was a cast member of *Saturday Night Live,* so he was gone a lot of the time. Sarah Jessica Parker was also off working a good deal, and when those two were back in town, it was Kiefer who was away. So while they were technically all living in the same place, they were actually rarely all together.

"It was a really strange, wonderfully surreal time," Sutherland remembers. "It was like we were all living a real-life Melrose Place for actors. We drifted in and out, going on location and then returning. Whoever was there would look after everything, like taking care of Sarah's cats. I would end up living there with them for almost three years." And Sutherland never paid a dime in rent during the whole time he lived there. Why not? "Because they never asked me to," he says.

Kiefer soon hit the road to Reno, Nevada, and then to Utah for the location shoot of his next film. *Promised Land* is a drama about two high-school friends who leave their hometown and go out into the world with high expectations, only to return home when life doesn't turn out so well. Davey Hancock (played by Jason Gedrick) is a former basketball star who drops out of college and becomes a local policeman. Rivers, who leaves town with high political ambitions, turns into a virtual drifter and comes back in disgrace to face his dying father.

With *Promised Land*, Kiefer Sutherland confirmed that he could handle just about any kind of role: good guys, bad guys, good guys that end up bad—anything. He was still in his teens, and it looked like he had all the makings of a Hollywood success story. He had youth, energy, and above all an intense professional drive for perfection.

This impressed even his father: "He did come to me one night when I was living in Los Angeles. He stood at the end of the bed and he said, 'Can I do my audition for you?' And I was, 'Oh God, puh-lease, oh, dear. Okay.,' And he did it, and it was brilliant. I was so relieved. And he said, 'Well, that's the way they want me to do it. Can I show you how I want to do it? And so he did it again, completely different. And it was way better. My hair stood up. I don't even remember whether he got the part, but I knew he'd be okay. He was wonderful."

6

THE LOST BOY

"I'll tell you, 1987 was a big year for me in a lot of ways. What I did in that year changed everything from there on in, for the rest of my life."

–Kiefer Sutherland

The year 1987 was a watershed for Sutherland. While he continued to act in films with intriguing scripts that challenged him as an actor, he also accepted a role in a major Hollywood studio film that would take him from being just a talented newcomer to a bona fide Hollywood movie star. After this, when his name appeared on lists of actors to cast in big-budget projects, studio executives no longer said, "What has he done, again?" They now started to say, "Yes, sign Kiefer if you can."

Nevetheless, not every role was for him. In 1987, Stephen Herek, who had made one low-budget horror movie called *Critters,* connected with a couple of hot writers named Ed Solomon and Chris Matheson to write a script about two layabouts named Bill and Ted who, in an effort to pass a history test, stumble through misadventures in time that bring them into contact with major historical figures. This was a goofy, stoner parable that seemed a good fit for the youth-oriented film atmosphere of the times.

Every young actor in town was trying to get a meeting or a reading for the roles of Bill and Ted, including Sutherland. "We were seeing a lot of young actors for the roles," says Herek. "We didn't know what we were looking for in terms of physical make up; we just knew what we were looking for in terms of attitude and presentation." When Sutherland came in to talk to him about the role of Ted Logan, Herek knew he had the chops, but there was something "not Ted" about him. "Kiefer could not play dumb," says Herek. "When you looked at him, even though he was interesting, he always had that glimmer of sarcasm, that knowing look of intelligence about him." But dumb was what they needed, so Sutherland was rejected. Keanu Reeves ended up playing Ted, and Alex Winter ended up playing Bill.

The mid-eighties was a wonderful time for screenwriters. All of a sudden, spec screenplays—screenplays written without a contract then put out into the marketplace to see if any producer or studio would buy them—were commanding record fees. The frenzy began when a young writer named Shane Black wrote a screenplay about a crazy L.A. cop called *Lethal Weapon* and sold it to Warner Bros. for over $1.4 million. The 1987 film was a hit, earning over $120 million worldwide, and turned into a huge franchise with three more films in the series raking in a total of almost a billion dollars. Black would later earn millions more for the 1991 Bruce Willis flop *The Last Boy Scout*. Other screenwriters benefitted just as much. The prolific Joe Eszterhas boasted he made $3 million for his *Basic Instinct* screenplay when it was nothing more than a premise scribbled on a cocktail napkin. It was in this giddy atmosphere that the screenwriting team of Janice Fischer and James Jeremias were able to sell their screenplay called *The Lost Boys* to Warner Bros. It was not a record-setting sale—in the mid-six-figure range—but it was far more than the pair ever expected to get.

The Lost Boys was the type of big-studio project that seems conceived in chaos at first, taking years to develop and, going through innumerable changes in script and personnel , delays, and personal rivalries, only to finally emerge as a huge hit in theaters and subsequently be hailed as a masterpiece of creative planning.

The screenplay in its original form was a darkish take on J.M. Barrie's story of Peter Pan, whose never-aging band of companions is called the Lost Boys. The lost boys in the original Fischer-Jeremias screenplay are all goofy kids in the fifth and sixth grade. The twist is that they happen to be vampires. Richard Donner was originally slated to direct the film, but in the end he decided not to. "I passed on *The Lost Boys*, yes, but I really just passed on directing it," Donner says. "The early draft of the screenplay was quite different and read more like a action-comedy-horror version of a film I had already made called *The Goonies*. But I liked the writers, and I liked the energy and the idea behind the script; I said I would come on board to get it into shape for another director so the picture could get made. I was really busy at the time with back-to-back projects, so even if I did want to direct the film once it was developed and rewritten, I was already off on my next thing." As it happens, that next thing was the above-mentioned *Lethal Weapon*. In the meantime, Donner signed on as executive producer of *The Lost Boys* and used his considerable clout with Warner Bros. to make sure the film succeeded.

Mary Lambert, who had directed a few films but was mostly known for her work on some of Madonna's early music videos, was brought in, but her sensibilities immediately clashed with the Hollywood studio mentality. She left shortly after being hired due to "creative differences," and would later direct the horror hit *Pet Sematary*.

Warner Bros. and Executive Producer Donner then approached Joel Schumacher to direct the film. Schumacher had directed only five films at the time (he has thirty to date) including his debut film, the stylish 1974 TV movie *The Virginia Hill Story,* about the gangster Bugsy Siegel's moll. Just before being offered *The Lost Boys,* he had directed the huge 1985 hit *St. Elmo's Fire.* Together with the late John Hughes's *The Breakfast Club,* released the same year, *St. Elmo's Fire* introduced to the public the group of young actors who came to be known as the Brat Pack.

Schumacher was interested, but only if the screenplay were rewritten to make the characters older teenagers. He wanted one of them to be a woman and demanded greater creative freedom to change the script in order to attract a much larger audience. The producers agreed, and screenwriter-for-hire Jeffrey Boam was brought in to do the overhaul. "I loved that film and I am glad that I held out for the changes," says Schumacher. "I could not have directed the film as written. I had no interest in it. But when the characters were made older, that brought in all sorts of new dimensions that excited me. From the love interest angle to the costumes to the motorcycles, it just felt a lot sexier to me that way. And it seems audiences completely agreed with me."

Once again Kiefer Sutherland was cast as a bad guy—David, the lead vampire, who wore black gloves and long black coats to go with his eerie, white-blond hair. "The glove thing was an add-on out of necessity," Sutherland reveals. "I was fucking around on one of the motorcycles and fell off and broke my arm. The glove I wore throughout the film was there simply to cover up the cast, but Joel made it look very cool, as he does everything."

The supporting cast included everyone from future Oscar-winner Dianne Wiest to Canadian kid actor Corey Haim to handsome leading-man-in-the-making Jason Patric. A young actress named Jami Gertz was cast as Star, the female vampire, and current reality-show-star Corey Feldman played the Rambo Jr.-type vampire hunter, Edgar Frog.

But the film that evolved belonged to director Joel Schumacher, a flamboyant former art director and costume designer, whose flashy, distinctive visual style makes his films truly dazzling. He has since shown that he can be low-key as well, and just as effectively. Schumacher cast Kiefer Sutherland as David because he felt that, while Kiefer was still a young man, he had a maturity about him. His voice sounded older than he was, his hairline was receding, and he could act. Schumacher would go on to cast Kiefer Sutherland in a number of other projects over the years, including his 2009 film *Twelve*. "Kiefer is a terrific actor who wears his demons on his sleeve," Schumacher says. "That's what makes him a very interesting artist to watch . . . Kiefer isn't afraid of looking ugly, of looking tired, of being a villain. He's afraid of being mediocre. He doesn't need the approval of the audience the way some stars do."

The Lost Boys is the story of young brothers Michael and Sam, who, after their parents' painful divorce, move with their mother to the coastal California town of Santa Clara to live with her eccentric father, played by the wonderfully versatile character actor Barnard Hughes. Santa Clara is a peculiar town that is dominated by a gang of young people who appear only at night and who dress in odd clothes that make them look like modern-day pirates. As the young brothers soon find out, the town is infested with vampires, and this group of young people, led by the white-haired, charismatic David, is the main group of them. David's girlfriend is the mysterious Star, and it is through her that the older brother, Michael, is invited to the group's hangout, an old hotel that was all but destroyed in an earthquake. There, still unaware of exactly who these people are, Michael participates in a strange ceremony and inadvertently becomes a vampire initiate, a "half" vampire.

Sam has met and befriended a couple of goofy brothers who know about the vampires and have made it their mission to discover where they sleep and to destroy them. When Sam discovers Michael's condition, they go after the overall head vampire, an older vampire called Max, in order to kill him and return Michael to a fully human condition.

The Lost Boys was released to over a thousand North American screens on July 31, 1987, and grossed over $32 million domestically, a good return for an R-rated horror film. The big winners in the film were Jason Patric, who played Michael and was carrying his first big film, and Kiefer Sutherland, once again a scene stealer, who left a resonating impression on audiences. Sutherland had a great time. "It was the first of many terrific working experiences I was to have with Joel Schumacher. I remember relaxing and having a good time with this one. Playing David the vampire was just a fun time. I got to dress up in wicked clothes, ride motorcycles, have a great girl, and had terrific actors to play off of. It was a lot of fun."

Sutherland released two minor efforts in 1987 as well: *Crazy Moon,* a small Canadian production, and *The Killing Time,* in which he plays a deranged killer, the first of many. The character, listed only as "The Stranger" in the credits, murders a man on a highway. The dead man was on his way to a small border town in California where he had been hired as a deputy sheriff. The killer steals the man's identity and heads on to the town to assume the post as deputy. When he arrives in town, however, he himself becomes the target of a murder plot when the sheriff and his girlfriend plot to kill her husband and frame the new deputy for the crime. Sutherland once again reveled in his role, playing another lunatic psychopath who is as charismatic as he is unhinged.

This film would just be a footnote in Sutherland's career were it not for the young actress playing the sheriff's wife. Pretty, dark-haired Camelia Kath played the role of Laura Winslow. Kath was the widow of Terry Kath, one of the founding members of the band Chicago. She arrived on screen with a dazzling broad smile and beautiful eyes. In September 1986, while still filming, Sutherland and Kath began dating and showed up at restaurants and social functions together. At the time, Kiefer Sutherland was twenty and Camelia Kath was thirty-two.

Sutherland and Kath became very close despite their age difference, and the relationship turned passionate. They married on September 12, 1987, almost a year to the day after they began dating. The marriage was Kiefer's idea, and he was excited about it, but naturally he was also nervous. It was one of the few occasions in his life when he sought out the advice of his father. "I asked him about it when we were taking a walk together around the property he had in Quebec. It was a huge and stunningly beautiful place he had there," adds Sutherland. "I told him that I was really in love with this woman and wanted to marry her—for all the right reasons, I thought. But still I was freaked out a bit by the prospect. I could see that he was on the fence about what kind of advice to give me, so he went for positive reinforcement and told me that it would be great, but that I had to adore my wife and enjoy pleasing her and taking care of her every minute of the day. I thought it was really bad advice I was getting from him, but I also never loved my father more than when he was giving it. He was trying to be supportive and share in my joy and enthusiasm."

Sutherland ended 1987 on top of the world. He had become a major movie star, had a new wife, and his prospects for the next year were very promising. His star was definitely rising in the Hollywood heavens. He was now a name actor in his own right, but he was not seen yet as one who could yet carry a film by himself. A pattern was developing: a big production followed by lesser efforts. But he was young, just twenty-one, and was pushing awfully hard on all fronts. Ever an intense actor, he held to a strict code of professionalism in his work, but he had to blow off steam sometime. As his career grew, so did his drinking and his personal recklessness. And he didn't hide it. Even though there were a lot of eyes on him. It was as if, though now, it was as if he werewas daring people to accept him as he was.

YOUNG GUN

"I embarrass my daughter, I embarrass my mother, and I embarrass myself. I know that I am doing it. I regret doing it. But I still keep on doing it."

–Kiefer Sutherland

Riding the wave of success that *The Lost Boys* brought him, Sutherland now found himself on the receiving end of numerous film offers. He no longer needed to take whatever came along and try to make the best of it—he could now pick and choose.

Before he would be completely free to accept the higher-profile projects coming his way, however, he needed to conclude an earlier commitment to another film. This project was a film called *1969*, which he had accepted in order to work with his pal and roommate Robert Downey Jr. The film tells the story of two friends, Scott and Ralph, who live in a small town during the height of the Vietnam War. While Scott's brother enlists, Scott is staunchly anti-war. This causes a major rift in the family, especially between Scott and his father. Ralph and Scott decide to leave town for the summer in their van to experience the new freedoms of the Age of Aquarius. When they eventually return home, they learn of the death of Scott's brother in Vietnam. Shared grief brings the family closer together as father and son learn the true cost of war.

In early November 1987, *1969* went before the cameras. It was shot entirely on location in Savannah and Statesboro, Georgia, with additional filming in Hardeeville, South Carolina. The writer-director was Ernest Thompson, who had recently won an Oscar for his screenplay of *On Golden Pond*. He cast real-life friends Downey and Sutherland as Scott and Ralph and rounded out his cast with Bruce Dern, Winona Ryder, and Mariette Hartley.

The film is passionately rendered, well written, and well acted, but it is directed unevenly. The sixties, both culturally and visually, are perhaps the hardest of recent times to recreate effectively, and director Thompson only half succeeds. A strength of the film is the chemistry between the two leads. "I think the fact that Kiefer and I were very good friends off screen obviously allowed us a familiarity on screen," says Downey. "And what we also shared was this strange feeling that we were kind of playing our parents in the film, or at least our parents' sensibilities, because both Kiefer and I had parents who were fiercely against the war and who embraced that new freedom of the sixties. So that was kind of cool."

Initially *1969* had only a limited release, sneaking quietly into a couple of theaters in Los Angeles in August 1988. It got a much wider release in November of that year, however, after Sutherland and Downey had separately gained visibility from their other high-profile movies released in the interim. The film wound up making about $5 million domestically.

Downey had gained notice by appearing in two light comedies, *Rented Lips* and *Johnny Be Good*, in which he worked with his father—actor, writer, and director Robert Downey Sr. But Sutherland made a much bigger splash with his roles in *Bright Lights, Big City* and, especially, the very successful *Young Guns*.

Bright Lights, Big City was one of the higher-profile projects that made their way to Sutherland during this time. The novel of the same name on which the screenplay was based was written by Jay McInerney, a young New York novelist. As in Hollywood during this time, the New York literary scene also had a Brat Pack: a group of hot, young, twenty-something novelists who had debut bestsellers that brought them huge book contracts and public notoriety. The reaction to these young literary stars was effusive, even excessive. McInerney was praised as a contemporary of F. Scott Fitzgerald after *Bright Lights, Big City*—his first novel—came out. The book described the fast, hedonistic cocaine-strewn lives of young New Yorkers in the 1980s and was praised by reviewers for the way it captured the essence of the city at the time.

The main character in the book is Jamie Conway, a disillusioned writer who uses drugs, sex, and clubbing to avoid dealing with his personal problems. Originally, the role of Conway was slated for another hot young actor of the day, Tom Cruise. Cruise saw the value of the material, but ultimately turned the role down because he was uneasy with the character's casual drug use. The role was accepted by Canadian transplant, Michael J. Fox, another white-hot actor of the day. The co-lead, Jamie's rich, reckless friend Tad Allagash, went to fellow Canadian Kiefer Sutherland. Sutherland enjoyed himself in the role. "I loved that character; he was like me in a lot of ways, so I could channel a lot of demons through Tad."

The film was shot entirely in New York City, and the young cast, including Fox's future wife Tracy Pollan and the beautiful young actress Phoebe Cates, took full advantage of this as they thoroughly sampled the city's wild club scene. Michael J. Fox noted the uncomfortable parallel between the movie they were filming and the lives of the actors off-set. "There is something heady, something very dangerous about being in New York and working on a big, high-profile film, the world at your feet, and being that young. That combination of things led to some great times but also pushed a few of us perilously close to completely losing ourselves in our own self-indulgences." There is little doubt that Fox was speaking mainly about Sutherland.

Bright Lights, Big City was released on April 1, 1988, and pulled in a rather limp $5.1 million on its opening weekend, despite being released on almost 1,200 screens. It went on to gross only about $16 million during its domestic run, far short of its budget of $25 million. Despite the box office disappointment, Sutherland once again came out okay. The performances were not the reason audiences rejected it; they were uniformly good. The critic Roger Ebert, for instance, thought that *Bright Lights, Big City* contained some of the best work Michael J. Fox had ever done on film. For his part, Sutherland turned in a wry and sardonic performance, making his character both captivating yet repulsive. When Tad chastises the tardy Jamie with the line that there were "dances to be danced, drugs to be hoovered, and women to be Allagashed," Sutherland delivers a perfect line, making the audience love the guy while thinking him a complete jerk at the same time.

* * * *

The next role Sutherland accepted took him from the excesses of 1980s New York to the great spaces of the nineteenth-century Wild West. *Young Guns* marked a high point in Sutherland's early career. It was one of his biggest, most popular successes before his turn to television and *24* many years later. But it was also the end of his career's adolescence. The meteoric rise of this burgeoning star, who after all was only twenty-one, necessarily was going to plateau, and despite possessing the professional maturity of someone much older, Sutherland's struggle would have to switch from merely making himself known to adjusting the momentum of his career and his personal life to ward a sustainable pace. This is difficult for any young actor, but for a personality like Sutherland's this was doubly so. His creativity was nurtured by an intensity in his craft and in his life, and despite sincere attempts to establish personal stability, his own drive as an artist actually stood in his way. Yet, it was on the set of this film that awoke another passion, one that much later, and indirectly, not just saved his career, but made it.

* * * *

Young Guns was written by a movie-star-handsome young man named John Fusco, another of the fortunate screenwriters to ride the wild wave of the screenplay marketplace of the mid- to late 1980s. Fusco, a free spirit, dropped out of school at sixteen to tour the American South and made money to live on by playing blues in bars. He used that experience to write his first screenplay, an autobiographical effort called *Crossroads*. Director Walter Hill made the movie of Fusco's screenplay, and the film not only became a cult classic but was also the inspiration for the video game Guitar Hero III—Legends of Rock.

Fusco then turned his talents and imagination to the American West. The result was *Young Guns,* a revisionist spin on the legend of Billy the Kid. In Fusco's version, Billy the Kid leads a pack of young gunslingers, all of whom have been deputized, to seek justice in the case of a rancher who has been murdered. The rancher, John Tunstall, had sheltered and educated the young men, and they all had looked up to him as a father figure. But the deputies abuse their authority when they kill the men they arrest for the crime. The deputies then become the hunted ones.

Fusco's screenplay was snapped up quickly as a natural vehicle for the young actors who were hot at the time. Some critics would sardonically dismiss the film as *Young Guns: the Brat Pack on Horseback.* And that's not entirely unfair. A young filmmaker on the rise, Christopher Cain, was hired to direct the film, and Cain thought his friend Emilio Estevez would be a perfect Billy the Kid. Estevez had starred in Cain's 1985 feature *That Was Then . . . This Is Now,* for which Estevez had adapted the screenplay from the S.E. Hinton novel of the same name.

Sutherland co-starred in the role of Josiah Gordon "Doc" Scurlock, a bespectacled New York City teacher turned dead-eye gunfighter. The character is clearly based on the legendary Doc Holliday, the dentist turned gunfighter who rode with Wyatt Earp and his brothers. This was one of the more colorful roles in a film that was filled with eccentric, well-struck characters played by some very good actors. The role of the Native American member of the gang of six, José Chavez y Chavez, was assigned to Lou Diamond Phillips, who became a close friend of Sutherland's. They worked together several more times throughout their careers, and much later, Phillips's daughter would even play opposite Kiefer on *24*. Charlie Sheen, Dermot Mulroney, and Casey Siemaszko filled the rest of the six leads, and the veteran actors Terence Stamp, Jack Palance, and Terry O'Quinn, of subsequent *Lost* fame, rounded out the cast.

Terence Stamp remembers *Young Guns* fondly. "There is something magical about doing an American Western film. I had done a couple before, of course, but this one was like a pure old-fashioned Western. What I took away from that film, though, was a great admiration for the new generation of young screen actors, especially Emilio and Kiefer. Kiefer had an intensity about him and an instinct about acting that was far beyond his years."

Filming of *Young Guns* began in New Mexico on February 8, 1988, and continued through the end of March. Sutherland had to leave the set briefly ten days into shooting to rush home to be with his wife Camelia Kath as she was giving birth to the couple's daughter, Sarah Jude. But once mother and infant were settled on the home front, he returned to the set. The film used locations all over northern New Mexico, from Santa Fe to Ojo Caliente to Tesuque Pueblo. Sutherland loved the landscape. "I don't know if it's because I'm from Canada, where we're used to wide open spaces, or just because I needed a change of scenery, but the western United States just had me in a perpetual state of awe at its natural beauty."

Lou Diamond Phillips declared in 1999 that *Young Guns* was one of his favorite films. "It is a cowboy movie, man," he said. "It was great fun to dress up in those clothes and carry six-guns and ride horses and explore that American mythos. Kiefer and I hit it off right away. I think we both recognized in each other a kind of older soul inhabiting a younger man. After *Young Guns* was finished we immediately started looking for other things to do together on screen."

For Phillips, the "American mythos" of the West may have been about dressing up and toting six-guns, but for Sutherland something more profound was happening. It began with horses: "I'm not sure what it was. I just really found it a wonderful, natural high to be on a horse and riding. On *Young Guns,* I never wanted to get off my horse; the riding scenes were the ones that I enjoyed the most."

Young Guns was released on August 12, 1988, and made $7 million its first weekend, more than half its modest $13 million budget. It went on to make well over $45 million domestically, and in Hollywood, when a movie becomes that kind of a bona fide hit, the next step is often inevitable: a sequel. But before that could happen, Sutherland had another couple of films to make.

He also had to adjust to life as a new father at just shy of twenty-two-years old, alongside a thriving career and a public persona that was growing by the week. "I wanted to be older than I was, faster than I was naturally getting there. There I was, a very young man with a wife and a child and a house and a very busy career. But I was still giving in to those impulses that successful guys naturally give in to now and then—only I was giving into them often. I thought I could handle it all."

Since Hollywood is the great enabler of excesses, especially when one is making money for others, Sutherland's behavior was either excused or covered up. But it was not just that he was starting to get a dubious reputation. It was apparent to all, except perhaps himself, that he could behave this way only so long before something had to give.

8

JULIA

"I commend Julia for seeing how young and silly we were, even at the last minute, even as painful and as difficult as it was. Thank God she saw it."

–Kiefer Sutherland

After *Young Guns* came a contemporary cop movie called *Renegades,* which teamed Sutherland again with Lou Diamond Phillips. Writer David Rich sold his first screenplay with this story of an undercover cop. Buster McHenry, played by Sutherland, investigates police corruption and consequently is not at all popular inside the force. While undercover on his current case, McHenry is involved in a heist that goes terribly wrong and is wounded. During the robbery an ancient spear is taken. Phillips's character, Hank Storm, is a Native American who wants to get his tribe's spear back. McHenry wants to find the people who shot him. After some initial conflict, the two men team up together to find what each is looking for.

Renegades was shot in Philadelphia and Toronto in early 1989. Director Jack Sholder had this to say about working with Sutherland: "What I like about

Kiefer as an actor is that he can play a lead and carry a film or he can be a very effective ensemble actor; whatever the role requires is within his capabilities. In this film, he is asked to play a basically decent guy who just gets pulled off track all the time. In this story, he decides to do the right thing, no matter what it takes." Phillips was equally admiring. "Kiefer and I connect on screen. When that happens it is probably best not to try to figure out why or overanalyze it, because then you will be constantly trying to work towards that thing rather than just letting it happen organically."

Sutherland sported a moustache in this film to try to look a bit older. At twenty-three, he was playing a veteran undercover officer close to burning out. *Renegades* also featured *Lost Boys* star Jamie Gertz in the female lead, as well as a young actor named Rob Knepper, who many years later found success on television as a co-star in the very popular series *Prison Break.*

* * * *

Anyone who has ever been on a movie set knows full well just how unglamorous and tedious and downright boring is. There are hours of setting up lights and dolly tracks and blocking out camera moves, followed by a just a few minutes of shooting. Then the whole process begins all over again. On the Toronto shoot of *Renegades,* that tedium was increased fivefold by the complexity of rigging special-effects scenes and pyrotechnics for several night shoots.

There was a young woman working on the set of *Renegades* as a set production assistant who got to know Kiefer Sutherland during that shoot. Often she would wait with him as the special effects were rigged and re-rigged. "The thing I remember about my conversations with Kiefer was how complex a guy he is," she says. "I remember one night he seemed pretty bummed out, so I asked him what was wrong, and he told me that he was a new father and was nervous about that; he said that it was something he felt wonderful about but felt ill equipped to do." She tried to reassure him, telling him that every new father has those feelings, has that anxiety, it is perfectly natural. "He said that it had been suggested that he try therapy to deal with the way shehe grew up, but he didn't think he needed it. It was just the life of a family of actors, and t. That life involves being away on location, going where your work is. But he feared the effect that would have on his child."

The production assistant rememberse being with Sutherland when a journalist asked him about his reputation as a wild partier and drinker. "He smiled at this woman and shook his head and, he then looked at me with an expression that said, 'see what I have to put up with?' He then told her, 'Look, I like to drink a little, I like to smoke, I like to enjoy the off- hours I have with friends. I have no problems with any of that. And if any of it does gets to be a problem for me, I'm pretty sure I will be the first to know it.' "

Or perhaps not. Later that year, Sutherland was arrested for driving under the influence and carrying a loaded and concealed weapon. In return for pleading no contest to alcohol-related reckless driving, the other charges were dropped, however. He was lucky. But there is no evidence that he even attempted to change his behavior as a result of this first brush with the law.

* * * *

Renegades was released to tepid reviews on June 2, 1989. Siskel and Ebert slaughtered the movie on their TV review show, judging it nothing more than crass commercialism, without originality or ambition. Nevertheless, it pulled in just under $8 million domestically—not a bomb, but nowhere near the success that *Young Guns* and *Lost Boys* had been.

Expectations were higher for Sutherland's next film. *Flashback* tells the story of '60s activist Huey Walker, a wanted man who has been in hiding for twenty years. Walker is played by Dennis Hopper, the quintessential '60s hippie actor. When he is finally apprehended, a young FBI agent named John Buckner, played by Sutherland, is assigned to escort Walker across country by train for his trial. Unfortunately, Buckner is not very streetwise and while riding on the train, Walker spikes the agent's mineral water with LSD. After Agent Buckner starts tripping out, Walker steals his identity—he cuts his hair, shaves his beard, dresses in Buckner's suit and wears his badge. Walker then keeps Buckner on a perpetual high until Walker can get to a safe haven.

The identity switch has been a staple of Hollywood comedy since movies began, but what sets this film apart is the way the two actors interact. Dennis Hopper plays his role with just the right amount of tongue-in-cheek—he was himself, of course, a grand icon of the '60s counterculture. He even references himself in the film, saying, "It takes more than going down to your local video store and renting *Easy Rider* to be a rebel."

Sutherland's Buckner turns out to have been raised by hippie parents. He was a little hippie who just wanted to be like other kids, so he grows up to become the sort of straight-laced type that his parents had warned him against. Sutherland has a wonderful series of scenes where he talks about how much he hated being the kid who ate alfalfa sprouts and wore tie-dyed clothing and where he breaks down and cries while watching family home movies from the sixties.

Flashback arrived in theaters on February 2, 1990. Though it was a much better movie than *Renegades,* it only pulled in just over $6 million at the domestic box office and Paramount Pictures considered it a major disappointment. But the movie is better than its public reception suggests. The reviews that Sutherland got for his work, in particular, were uniformly positive, and film critic Roger Ebert complimented Sutherland for underplaying the role to perfection.

* * * *

By 1990, while the public's response to his films varied, Sutherland himself was receiving good reviews. He was still quite young, but his career was progressing beyond those of his fellow Brat Pack actors. They, for the most part, were stuck in teen angst movies or limp sex comedies, whereas Sutherland had carved out a well-rounded film career with some careful choices.

But on the home front, things were in complete disarray. By the end of 1989, he had already been separated from his wife, Camelia Kath, for several months, and on February 1, 1990, they officially divorced. Their daughter, Sarah Jude, would stay with her mother. Sutherland was all of twenty-three. "It was my fault, all of it. I wanted to be a grown-up too fast. I wanted to feel I had arrived, and I went about that in all the wrong ways. But we did have a beautiful daughter together, and we have remained friends. Despite all my failings, there was good that came out of it."

Perhaps it was the emotional turmoil surrounding the separation and divorce, but Sutherland stumbled in his next project, a Dennis Potter-ish film called *Chicago Joe and the Showgirl.* Shot in England, the film is a fanciful and ambitious movie based loosely on the true story of what was called the "cleft chin" murder case in 1944. Director Bernard Rose referred to the movie before its official release as the best British film ever made. This turned out to be rather imprudent, as the film was a huge flop and received the worst critical drubbing Sutherland had ever been associated with.

The plot concerns an AWOL American serviceman named Karl Hulten hanging out in London during World War II. While dealing on the black market, he meets Betty Jones, a wild-eyed stripper who infatuates him. To impress her, Hulten pretends he is Chicago Joe, a front man for American gangsters looking to expand into the U.K. Jones, for her part, lives in a fantasy world constructed around Hollywood movies. She attaches herself to Joe and prods him into committing a series of petty crimes, which escalate rapidly until the couple commits murder.

Sutherland comes off badly in the film. His Hulten is weak and gullible as he is manipulated by his flamboyant lover, played by Emily Lloyd. It seems as though Sutherland, in choosing again to underplay his character, perhaps to avoid upstaging his co-star, only succeeded in making an already meek character boring. He didn't regret the experience though. "I don't think I chose wrong at all. It was a terrific script, and the director was an interesting guy with ambitious ideas. Going in, it all looked solid. But you can just never tell how things will come together in the end; you can never tell if what you are offering up is going to interest an audience."

The film was released in the United States and Canada on July 29, 1990. On its opening weekend, it was shown in only six theatres and made less than $15,000. In all, it appeared in no more than eighteen theaters and only grossed a little over $85,000 domestically. Sutherland quickly shook off the flop, however. He had already returned to Los Angeles to resume his life as a movie star.

* * * *

The period of the richly priced spec screenplay was coming to an end by the late 1980s, but there were still some big deals to be had. Peter Filardi was an inexperienced writer with only one professional credit to his name, as an episode writer of *McGyver,* when he wrote *Flatliners.* His screenplay was about a group of brilliant medical students who experiment with inducing clinical death and then resuscitating each other in order to discover what lies beyond life. Gradually, in their temporary deaths, they begin to see ghosts from their early lives and are forced to confront them to resolve the past.

The screenplay caught the attention of actor Michael Douglas and his producing partner, Rick Bieber. They bought it for development through their company Stonebridge Entertainment, which had a production deal with Columbia Pictures. Besides being a terrific actor, Michael Douglas is probably an even better producer. He won an Academy Award for Best Picture on his very first outing as a producer, *One Flew Over the Cuckoo's Nest.* In *Flatliners,* Douglas saw a potential commercial hit; with the right cast of actors, he felt it could be a hip gothic-horror tale set in contemporary times.

Director Joel Schumacher agreed to do the film, but as with *The Lost Boys,* only if he were given room to use his unique and eccentric visual flair to create a truly distinctive movie. Indeed, the medical school where the students study looks more like the inside of a gothic cathedral, and Schumacher uses carefully controlled lighting effects for each character in order to reflects each's individual sensibilities.

Schumacher's first casting decision was to choose his *The Lost Boys* star Kiefer Sutherland for the lead role Nelson, the most brilliant and daring of the medical students. "Kiefer was my only real pre-determined casting choice," he reports. "I had hoped to get Julia Roberts, but I knew that Kiefer was the actor who would anchor this film."

The rest of the cast was made up of other actors on the rise. Some already knew the taste of success, while others were hoping *Flatliners* would be their big break. Julia Roberts was just another fledgling actor when she signed on, but before the production was finished that had changed. When the massive hit *Pretty Woman* was released in March 1990, in which she co-starred with Richard Gere, she was suddenly one of the hottest actresses in Hollywood. *Flatliners* co-star Kevin Bacon already had a huge hit under his belt with 1984's *Footloose*. William Baldwin was looking for a big role that would break him out, although he too had just made a fantastic movie with Richard Gere called *Internal Affairs*. And Oliver Platt, the recognizable face that that filmgoers often struggle to put a name to, rounded out the main cast.

The performances of Kiefer Sutherland and Julia Roberts dominate this movie. Sutherland's character, Nelson, is perfectly arrogant and driven, passionate and intense, and he sets the tone of the film with his very first line: "Today is a good day to die." This time, Sutherland chose not to underplay the character; brashness was what made Nelson believable. "I thought *Flatliners* was a smart and provocative film," Sutherland says. "But it still was an entertaining and thrilling ride. That was what interested me about it. Plus, I knew Joel Schumacher would give it an unforgettable look."

The narrative loses a bit of steam when it moves from its depiction of the competitive natures of the characters to the more existential storyline about redemption and forgiveness, but all in all, *Flatliners* is a smart, very commercial, big-Hollywood-studio movie. It was released on August 10, 1990, and was an enormous hit; it cost around $26 million to produce and grossed almost $70 million domestically.

With *Flatliners,* the arc of Sutherland's career was on the rise again. Here he was essentially carrying the movie, and that was a change. The accolades he received were well deserved, but timing had helped: he shared top billing with the hottest actress of the moment and their relationship on and off the screen set Hollywood's imagination on fire. It was an peak, enviable moment. And for a number of diverse and, unrelated reasons, none of it would last.

* * * *

As soon as *Flatliners* wrapped, Sutherland headed off to shoot *Young Guns II,* the sequel to his biggest hit to date. From January 19 through the end of March 1990, as his divorce was being finalized, he was on location in New Mexico and Arizona. Sutherland again played Doc Scurlock, Emilio Estevez returned as Billy the Kid, and Lou Diamond Phillips also reprised his role as Chavez y Chavez. There were also some additions to the cast. Christian Slater appeared as a character called Arkansas Dave Rudabaugh, and future *CSI* star William Peterson joined as Pat Garrett.

John Fusco wrote the film again, but this time Geoff Murphy was tapped as director. The film was released on August 1, 1990, a week before *Flatliners.* Although *Young Guns II* was a big hit, it wasn't quite as much fun as the first one. The film seemed to take itself too seriously, trying to capture some of the Sam Peckinpah-John Ford Western mythos instead of just playing it for a good time at the movies, the way the original had. The Brat Pack was that much older, and their attempt to join the ranks of established Western icons simply fell short. No longer teens, they were in an awkward period where as a group they weren't going to be taken seriously in the way the genre required.

* * * *

Sutherland took the "Western mythos" more seriously. His love of the West and of horses started during the making of *Young Guns* and was reinforced during *Young Guns II*. He went so far as to buy the horses he rode in those two films. Sutherland was so struck by the atmosphere of the West films that he decided to buy some land out there himself. But while those movies were made in the striking, arid landscape of northern New Mexico and Arizona, he was convinced by some Hollywood associates and by *Young Guns* screenwriter John Fusco that Montana was the place he should really look into.

In early 1989, he purchased some land near Whitefish, Montana, a thousand miles north of New Mexico, where several other Hollywood types had built vacation houses, beginning with Steve McQueen in the 1970s and among them Tom Cruise and another Young Gun, Emilio Estevez. For good reason, Montana is known as "Big Sky Country," and the area Sutherland chose, not far from Glacier National Park and the Canadian border, does not disappoint in this regard. Like any other newcomer, Sutherland set about tearing down the ramshackle buildings on his property and commissioned a brand-new house, one fit for an upcoming star.

* * * *

When Sutherland had finished work on location with *Young Guns II*, he returned to L.A. and to the new relationship he had begun with Julia Roberts. As he remembers it, he felt an instant attraction to Roberts when they met and began working together on *Flatliners*. But while they grew close during the shooting of the movie, it was not until after the film wrapped that they became an item. After Roberts's red-hot success in *Pretty Woman*, all of a sudden the romance that she and Sutherland were enjoying became front page news. Everywhere they went they were photographed and in no time at all the ups and downs of their new relationship became grist for the grocery-store-tabloid mill.

Sutherland said about Roberts at the time, "She is a vibrant, beautiful, smart, incredibly sexy woman with a fantastic laugh. Who wouldn't fall in love with her?" The infatuation was mutual, but, as he would admit much later, the relationship lacked a sustainable passion. The relationship took on a very public aspect, rising into the kind of giddy, other-worldly dimension experienced later by Ben Affleck and Jennifer Lopez, and Brad Pitt and Angelina Jolie. The frenzy mounted when *Flatliners* came out, where the public now saw the pair together in a monster hit film of their own.

Roberts and Sutherland announced their engagement in March 1991. Sutherland had moved in to Roberts's Hollywood Hills home and a date for the glitz wedding of the century was set: Friday June 14, 1991. The wedding would take place on a 20th Century Fox studio soundstage converted into a magical, garden-like setting. But the period between the engagement and the wedding day turned out to be not so magical. Stardom was having an effect on Julia Roberts. All of a sudden she was a big deal, and hordes of people began to surround her, to exploit her new-found fame.

The root of Roberts and Sutherland's very public split was hinted at as far back as February of 1991, when rumors started circulating that there was "another woman." Sutherland had been preparing for a role in a film that never made it to production, called *In from the Cold*. For his research, he had moved out of Roberts's house to live at the St. Francis Hotel, a flophouse in a decrepit neighborhood on Hollywood Boulevard. Across the street from the hotel was a pool hall, the Hollywood Billiards Parlor, just the kind of place where Sutherland liked to hang out. There Sutherland met Amanda Rice, and the two became drinking buddies. Then, so the rumors said, he started to visit her at the Crazy Girls Club, where she worked as a stripper and where he began to have epic, and ultimately public, drinking sessions. A story surfaced that had Sutherland and Rice taking their children together to Disneyland.

To top it off, as if Roberts and Sutherland's relationship were a set piece of theater for the public's entertainment, there was also "another man." A few years before meeting Sutherland, Roberts had met and dated Jason Patric, Sutherland's friend and co-star from *The Lost Boys*. Their romantic relationship lasted just a brief period, but their friendship seemed deep and genuine. In the early planning stages of the Sutherland-Roberts wedding, Patric was of course on the list of 150 invited guests. But just weeks before the wedding, his name was dropped from the list. At the time it was rumored that he had been dropped at the groom's insistence.

After his brief stint at the St. Francis Hotel, Sutherland returned to Roberts's house. The next few months seemed to be advance smoothly toward the wedding, but in mid-May the death knell sounded for the relationship: Amanda Rice sold her story to the tabloids. She divulged confidences that Sutherland had supposedly shared with her about Roberts: that she was insanely possessive and preoccupied with her looks, and that she had become a diva who believed her own press clippings.

Roberts took the tabloid story hard and just days later checked herself into a hospital. She ended up staying for almost a week. Her publicist released a statement that she had gone to the hospital for bad case of the flu. Sutherland made a public showing of his visits to Roberts and apparently charmed all the nurses and attendants on the floor. Meanwhile, he was publicly denying the stories being told by Amanda Rice. Sutherland's publicist, Annett Wolf, issued a statement to the effect that, yes, he knew Rice but had not had an affair with her.

On Roberts's return home, things appeared to move forward as planned. Her agent, Elaine Goldsmith, threw a bridal shower for Roberts that included her mother and a few school friends flown in from Georgia just for the party. Meanwhile, Sutherland headed to his recently built house in Montana to get it in shape for their honeymoon.

Roberts was given time off from her current big-budget film, Steven Spielberg's *Hook*, and headed to the Canyon Ranch Spa in Tucson, Arizona, for a bit of downtime.

Then, on June 9, just five days before the wedding was to take place, Roberts was spotted having dinner at the spa with none other than Jason Patric, and, according to *People* magazine, Patric appeared to be comforting her. Two days later, when she returned to Los Angeles, Roberts's publicist announced that the wedding was off—not officially cancelled just yet, but at least postponed. But shortly afterward it was clear that the engagement was over. It appeared to have been Roberts's decision alone; Sutherland only learned of it from a friend who had heard it on the news.

Sutherland took the whole thing hard. The Amanda Rice tabloid stories meant that people would think he had dumped America's newest sweetheart, when in fact it was he who had been dumped.

Even harder for Sutherland to swallow was that Roberts moved directly into the arms of another man. On the very day they were to have been married, Sutherland was moving his belongings out of Roberts's Hollywood Hills home while she was having lunch at L.A.'s Nowhere Café with Patric. After their meal, the pair headed to the airport and on to Ireland together. They checked into a Dublin hotel, but after hordes of reporters and photographers from the world over descended on the place, they left and were rumored to have headed to a home in Galway owned by Adam Clayton of the band U2.

While Sutherland's apparent relationship with Amanda Rice was often cited as the cause for the split, there was another side to the story. Julia Roberts, at twenty-three, already had a history of serial relationships and broken engagements. When she was just nineteen, she moved in with her boyfriend, Liam Neeson, who was thirty-five at the time. The two had just appeared together in a film called *Satisfaction*. After leaving that relationship, she fell in love with the actor who played her on-screen husband in *Steel Magnolias,* Dylan McDermott. When she met Sutherland on the set of *Flatliners* she broke off her engagement to McDermott to take up with him.

Looking back on the whole mess, Sutherland is gentlemanly. "I spent two years with her because I loved her, and she mattered more to me than anything at the time. I am not the easiest person to be with, and this all helped me to look at myself, which is hard. But she very cleverly said that she didn't think the marriage was the right thing. It was very brave of her to do that." And are his views about Jason Patric as forgiving? "We were friends, and I'm surprised that I never got a call from him. Instead, I heard about it from a stranger."

After the cancellation of the "Hollywood wedding of the year," Sutherland realized he was starting to tire of L.A. and Hollywood celebrity culture. His ranch in Montana was looking pretty good to him. "That was one of the things that caused Julia and I to split," Sutherland says. "I wanted to make good movies and do good work, but I wanted to live in Montana and raise horses when I wasn't doing that. Julia was all of a sudden the hottest actor on the planet and wanted to take that in and see where it took her. We enjoyed each other but were moving in different directions. There was a huge connection between us but . . . it was more like friends than the passionate relationship that she or I would have wanted. She saw that; I did not."

After the spilt Sutherland indeed retreated to Montana, but the memories of Roberts there were too strong—she and he had spent a lot of time there together—and he sold the place soon afterward.

9

A GOOD MAN

"I noticed that there was a change in the kind of movies I was being offered. I was still working, still able to work, but it just changed."

–Kiefer Sutherland

The last movie Sutherland released in 1990 was a cartoon. He did the voice-over for the title role in *The Nutcracker Prince,* a Canadian production. This very minor film marks a double turning point in Sutherland's career. The first change was that this was the first time he lent just his voice to a project. It is unclear why precisely he accepted the project, but the reason probably had to do with the second change: he had no other job offers. It turned out to be just a blip. Though the movie had been researching at the St. Francis Hotel, *In from the Cold,* never made it in production, by late spring 1991, after perhaps six months without work, he was busy with other, more substantial projects.

But for someone who had been working virtually non-stop since arriving in Hollywood for the last five years, this was a bit of a warning sign. It is a testament to Sutherland's survival skills, however, that he recognized his voice as an asset all by itself. Others had too, of course. The production assistant who became his confidant during the filming of 1989's *Renegades* denied ever becoming more involved with him, "But, that said, if you were to ask me if I would have become romantically entangled with Kiefer had that opportunity presented itself, that might require a different answer. He is a very charming guy, and that voice! I remember sitting around with him on the set, and he was speaking quietly to me. His voice has that power to almost lull you into an entranced state." The whole world, of course, now knows what she meant.

The idea of lending his voice to product advertising and animated films may have actually been inspired by his father. When the younger man found out just how much money his father, at a slow period in his own career, was earning by lending his distinctive voice to commercials, his mind started racing. "My dad does voiceover work for everything from Sunkist to Volvo. One day I thought, 'Hhmmm, that seems to be a good and easy way to make a living.'... So I gave Volvo a call one day and said, 'I do a really good Donald Sutherland. And I'll do it for half of what you pay him to do it.' " It was a joke, in the end, but Sutherland admits sheepishly, "I am not sure he has every forgiven me for that particular transgression. I am a bad son."

It is perhaps worth pointing out that *The Nutcracker Prince* also employed the talents of Peter O'Toole and Phyllis Diller, both once-big names but who at the time were no longer doing great things. This is common in Hollywood. Animated films and commercial voice-overs provide and other voice work provide a valuable nice stream of income for aging actors whose careers have fallen from previous heights. But Sutherland was only twenty-four.

* * * *

For his next live-action film, *Article 99*, Sutherland headed to Kansas City, Missouri. *Article 99* is about a group of doctors at a veterans' hospital who are overworked and frustrated by the stultifying bureaucracy all around them. The title refers to an insurance clause that says ex-soldiers may not be eligible for medical benefits if their injuries were not incurred during wartime or other military action. Taking their Hippocratic Oath to heart, these doctors decide to fulfill their responsibilities toward their patients, even if it means breaking hospital and government rules in the process. Sutherland plays Dr. Peter Morgan, an unorthodox but fiercely dedicated doctor. Ray Liotta, Forest Whitaker, Lea Thompson, and John McGinley are featured as other young doctors at the hospital.

It was while he was filming *Article 99* that Sutherland's plans to marry Julia Roberts crashed. His father was a great source of personal support during this time. "My dad was a great help to me during the whole marriage cancellation thing," Sutherland says. "He was in Los Angeles to be at the wedding, and when I saw him after the announcement that it was off, he just shook his head, put his hand on my shoulder, and said something like, 'Oh son . . .' " So, at one point in the film, Sutherland dons glasses and a fishing cap to become the spitting image of Hawkeye Pierce, paying homage to his father's role in *M*A*S*H.* It was a wink to his father, a subtle tribute from an appreciative son.

Article 99 was a well-written film that was solidly directed by Howard Deutch, who had made his debut with *Pretty in Pink* a few years before. Finally released in March 1992, *Article 99* probably would have earned a bigger audience were it not for distribution and marketing problems. The film was produced by Orion Pictures, which had been formed in 1978 by three executives at United Artists who had become frustrated by the interference of corporate bosses in the creative process.

Orion positioned itself as a so-called mini-major, meaning it was a small company willing to take on the major studios by producing films the larger companies wouldn't. Although Orion had made such Oscar-winning films as *Platoon, Dances with Wolves,* and *Silence of the Lambs,* the bulk of their films lost money, and the company was forced into bankruptcy in December 1991. Even Orion's successful films were highly leveraged, and their profitability was constrained by the profit-participation arrangements that Orion had made with actors and high-powered directors to lure them to the company in the first place. *Silence of the Lambs,* for example, was an enormous hit, but a lot of the money that came in as profit ended up being split among stars Jodie Foster and Anthony Hopkins and director Jonathan Demme.

As *Article 99* languished, Sutherland headed to Washington state to join the ensemble cast of *Twin Peaks: Fire Walk with Me.* Although his role was small, Sutherland said at the time that he would play any role in the film; he just wanted to work with director David Lynch. The film was shot from early September through early December of 1991, and like just about everything David Lynch does, the result was surreal and at times almost indecipherable. The television series on which this feature was based had been a cult hit, but Lynch's films are so imbued with his own eccentric sensibility that they rarely attract broad audiences. Consequently, despite its modest budget of $10 million, the film lost money.

****

It was around this time that Sutherland had another brush with the law for an alcohol-related offense. After a night of major drinking with pals, including fellow actor Gary Oldman, Sutherland was a passenger in a car with Oldman at the wheel. The police pulled them over for erratic driving. Oldman failed a field sobriety test and was arrested and forced to his knees as he was handcuffed. Sutherland, speaking to *Rolling Stone* magazine about the incident, said, "He [Oldman] was on his knees right level with the window of the car where I was. He had his head down and he looked up and he said, 'Right. Maybe next time we just have lunch.' That was the coolest kind of *Cool Hand Luke* line!" Oldman would battle with drinking for another couple of years before going into rehab in 1993. Sutherland, for his part, was completely unfazed by the incident.

* * * *

After completing his small role in *Twin Peaks,* Sutherland got a call from Rob Reiner, his first-ever Hollywood director, about a role in a film that would turn out to be the biggest hit Sutherland would ever appear in. Even better, this project gave him the chance to work with one of the icons of Hollywood stardom, Jack Nicholson.

A Few Good Men began as a play by Aaron Sorkin. The film rights to the play were sold before it had even been performed on stage, and Sorkin himself was hired to turn it into a screenplay—his first. The story centers around the investigation into the suspicious death of a young Marine at the American Marine base in Guantanamo Bay, Cuba. Sorkin, who would go on to create the television show *The West Wing,* was inspired by an incident he had heard about from his sister, a military attorney. A taut military courtroom drama, the film focuses on the pair of Navy attorneys brought in to defend two men accused of killing a fellow Marine while hazing him. The defendants claim that not only was the death accidental but that the hazing was done under direct orders.

A Few Good Men was to be Columbia Pictures' big release for the lucrative Christmas season in 1992. An industry rule of thumb is that big studio movies that are expected to make a lot of money are released in the summer season, while big studio movies that are expected to make a lot of money *and* get Golden Globe and Academy Award nominations are released during the Christmas season. With stars like Jack Nicholson, Tom Cruise, Kiefer Sutherland, and Demi Moore, together with writer Aaron Sorkin and director Rob Reiner, there was every reasonable expectation that nominations would come in for this one.

Director Rob Reiner was very fortunate in his casting. He got his first choices for the critical role of the commanding officer, Col. Nathan Jessup (Nicholson), and for the main Navy attorney, Lieutenant Junior Grade Daniel Kaffee (Cruise). Demi Moore was cast as the other Navy attorney, Lieutenant Commander Jo Anne Galloway, beating out Linda Hamilton, Elizabeth Perkins, and Helen Hunt, who also read for it.

Sutherland himself was hand-picked by director Rob Reiner for the role of First Lieutenant Jonathan Kendrick, a tough-as-nails Marine who operates as a kind of henchman for Nicholson's maniacally gung-ho Marine Commander Jessup. Highlighting the importance of his character, the words "And Kiefer Sutherland as Lt. Kendrick" appeared at the end of the opening credits. Sutherland is only in the film for a handful of scenes, but those scenes are crucial to the advancement of the plot.

Sutherland felt impressed and humbled around Nicholson. The veteran actor was asked to perform his famous "You can't handle the truth!" monologue a number of times so the director could cover the scene from different angles. Nicholson did the scene at full tilt over and over again, even when the camera was focused elsewhere. "Working with Nicholson was amazing. It was an incredible learning experience to watch him take command of his lines. Each time he did the scene he added something different. He was able to add dimension, even as he did it over and over."

There are a few Marines who probably don't have such fond memories of the shoot; early in the film, Sutherland's Lt. Kendrick is driving Kaffee and Galloway around the base in a Humvee. Sutherland had a hard time maneuvering the ultra-wide vehicle, and, several takes in a row, actually ran into some Marines. The vehicle was moving slowly and no one was injured, but it was a bit of an embarrassing day on the set for Sutherland.

Shot on a budget of $33 million, *A Few Good Men* was an enormous hit both critically and at the box office. During its theatrical run, it brought in almost a quarter of a billion dollars and was nominated for four Academy Awards, including best picture.

* * * *

Sutherland finished *A Few Good Men* in January 1992, and by April was back at work, this time on a big-budget remake of a chilling French-Dutch production called *The Vanishing*. The film is a rare example of a Hollywood remake where the director of the original film is brought in to direct the new version. But, as is often the case, the studio had a condition for the European director, George Sluizer: he could do the Hollywood remake only if he made the ending more upbeat. The producers felt the American public would never go for the bleakness of his original work.

In *The Vanishing*, a young couple, Jeff and Diane (Sutherland and Sandra Bullock), is on vacation. They stop at a roadside gas station, and Diane goes in to get something. Then she simply disappears. As times passes and no clues to her whereabouts surface, Jeff becomes obsessed with finding her, unaware he is being watched. Three years later, the watcher, a psychopathic chemistry teacher named Barney (Jeff Bridges), shows up at Jeff's apartment and admits he kidnapped Diane. He says if Jeff wants to find out what happened to her, he must allow himself to undergo what she did—be drugged and kidnapped.

Sutherland acquits himself well, but the movie itself was critically panned. Most reviewers compared the American version of *The Vanishing* negatively with Sluizer's Dutch version and its nihilistic ending. In *Spoorloos* ("without a trace"), the film ends darkly with the Jeff character buried alive, while Barney is never caught. In the Hollywood version, Jeff has a new woman in his life, Rita, played by Nancy Travis. When Jeff disappears, Rita finds and rescues him from where he is buried, whereupon Jeff tracks down and kills Barney. Everything is thus tied up neatly at the end, the way American audiences generally like them to be.

And that was it for a while. While he had just worked with David Lynch and Jack Nicholson, experiences many young actors in Hollywood would give their eye teeth for, Sutherland was dissatisfied. And rightly so. The roles he was being offered in big movies were small, and his major roles were in films that were decidedly minor. He felt unchallenged and unhappy. He knew he had to make some changes.

10

YOUNG SWORDS

"In the end, we all know what we've done."
–Kiefer Sutherland as Nelson in Flatliners

In an effort to shake things up, for his mood and for his career, Sutherland made the bold move of stepping behind the camera to direct a compelling made-for-television movie called *Last Light*.

Written by seasoned TV writer Robert Eisele, who also served as the film's executive producer, *Last Light* tells the story of two troubled characters, each of whom, despite his flaws, leads the other to personal redemption. In addition to directing the film, Sutherland also plays Denver Bayliss, a career criminal awaiting execution on death row. Forest Whitaker is Fred Whitmore, an ex-police officer turned prison guard who has a desperately unhappy home life with his wife and son. Bitter, withdrawn, and seeing nothing but failure in themselves, the men are wary of each other at first. As they interact, however, they gradually discover parallels in their lives and eventually come to an unspoken but deep understanding of each other. Bayliss, even as his execution date draws nearer, helps Whitmore come to terms with troublesome things in his past and leave them behind. Likewise, Whitmore helps Bayliss look back at his own wasted life and find enough peace to accept what is about to happen to him.

Last Light is an emotionally charged film that Sutherland directs with a surprisingly sure hand. He does not fall into the trap of many first-time directors by putting a heavy personal imprint on the material; he simply tells the story and lets the empathy in the script come through. He also takes the gutsy step of shooting the entire movie inside a real prison—California's Soledad Prison—a move that gives the film authenticity and a haunting emotional power as well.

Sutherland's co-star, Forest Whitaker, was impressed: "Kiefer directs very differently. I think he does it very well. The film works really well for me. He understands acting obviously, and I'm amazed he was able to act and direct at the same time, because he plays a pretty dark character. And he finished ahead of schedule and when we only had five weeks anyway." What was clear is that Sutherland brought to directing the same sort of professionalism that characterized him as an actor.

Even though his directorial debut was a critical success, Sutherland initially felt unsure of himself behind the camera. "I had always wanted to give directing a try. When I got the chance, I wanted to start with something that didn't come with a lot of commercial pressure because I was just feeling my way around. That's why I chose to do TV pieces for the first couple of things I directed." His father, on the other hand, was impressed with what his son was doing. "I am an actor, just an actor, and content to be so," says Donald Sutherland. "Kiefer is more of a filmmaker, a more diversely creative man than I ever was."

For his next acting job, Kiefer was back with a big studio, this time Disney. In the early part of 1993, two production companies, Disney and TriStar, were racing to cast Hollywood's hottest young actors for competing remakes of Alexandre Dumas's classic swashbuckling novel *The Three Musketeers*. Crucial to both companies, of course, was the casting of the three musketeers themselves. Disney had wanted Johnny Depp to play Athos, but he had turned them down in order to do the TriStar version to be directed by Jeremiah Chechik. Depp and Chechik had just worked together on the film *Benny and Joon,* for which Depp would be nominated for a Golden Globe for best actor. TriStar had offered the role of Porthos to Kiefer's *Flatliners* co-star Oliver Platt, but he had already accepted the same role in the Disney version. Among other actors considered for parts were Billy Baldwin and Gary Oldman, but both men were too busy. Disney went so far as to offer the role of d'Artagnan to Brad Pitt. But Pitt, who was just beginning his rise to superstardom after his roles in *Thelma and Louisa* and *A River Runs Through It,* turned them down. The part was then offered to Chris O'Donnell, who gladly snapped it up.

When the dust settled, the Disney version of the film came together first, and TriStar decided not to pursue its project. In Disney's liberally adapted screenplay, the three musketeers, Athos, Porthos, and Aramis, are all that is left of the elite King's Guards. The evil Cardinal Richelieu has disbanded the Guards, ostensibly so they can join the French army as it prepares for war against England. But the three musketeers refuse to step aside, suspecting correctly that Richelieu is planning to usurp the king's power. Richelieu assigns the job of dealing with the three holdouts to his henchman, the one-eyed and disgraced musketeer, Rochefort. But the musketeers receive help from a young French adventurer, d'Artagnan, who has traveled from the countryside to Paris to join the King's Guards.

The Disney film looked promising; it would be re-teaming *Young Guns* co-stars Sutherland and Charlie Sheen in the central roles of Athos and Aramis. There was a little confusion about the casting, though. While actor Cary Elwes joined Sutherland and Sheen in giving pre-production interviews in New York about their respective roles in *The Three Musketeers,* ultimately Elwes wasn't cast in the film at all. He would appear instead in Mel Brooks's *Robin Hood: Men in Tights.*

The adaptation of Dumas's classic was done by David Loughery, the screenwriter for *Flashback.* The film's director was Stephen Herek, who had just scored a major hit for Disney with *The Mighty Ducks,* starring another *Young Guns* alumnus, Emilio Estevez. Casting was rounded out with an interesting mixture of women in the lead female roles. Rebecca DeMornay, of *Risky Business* fame, played the main female lead, Milady de Winter; Gabrielle Anwar played Queen Anne; and French star Julie Delpy played Constance, d'Artagnan's love interest. Tim Currey was Cardinal Richelieu, and Canadian actor Michael Wincott played Rochefort.

Sutherland, Oliver, and O'Donnell were required to undergo six weeks of sword-fighting and fencing training prior to principal photography. Charlie Sheen missed out on the training, however, because he was still shooting another film at the time, and only joined the cast on set later. *The Three Musketeers* went before the cameras in England in April 1993, then headed to Austria, where the bulk of the film was shot. When Sheen finally made it to the location, it was widely reported that he and brother-in-arms Sutherland enjoyed many of the local bars and hotspots, not necessarily endearing themselves to the locals in the process. According to one report, Sutherland and Sheen were so drunken and rowdy while on location in Austria that one tavern banned them.

Sheen and Sutherland have had curious parallels in their careers, from public misbehavior to serious professional success. Currently they hold the distinction of being the top two highest-paid actors on television, with Sutherland at number one with his staggering contract for *24* and Sheen coming in second for his starring role in the show *Two and A Half Men*. There was a bit of a duel between their agents regarding the credits for *The Three Musketeers*; in the end, Sheen got top billing, but Sutherland's image was bigger and more central on the movie poster. Nevertheless, the two seemed to be having a fine time together.

Shooting lasted until the beginning of August 1993 and the film arrived in theaters three months later, on November 12. While the film looked good, it was apparent that the casting hadn't worked; the actors didn't seem to truly inhabit the movie. Chris O'Donnell played d'Artagnan with an accent more appropriate to Malibu than rural France. Charlie Sheen's sloppy enunciation was painful. The only two actors who attempted to put at least a mid-Atlantic spin on their delivery were Michael Wincott and Kiefer Sutherland, the two Canadians. And poor Julie Delpy, who is French, actually had to Americanize her French pronunciation so it wouldn't be in such startling contrast to the others.

Despite the power of the Disney name, *The Three Musketeers* was not well received. A number of major critics, Roger Ebert among them, asked whether there was even a need for yet another version of *The Three Musketeers*, and Leonard Maltin dubbed the film "Young Swords" in a nod to *Young Guns* alumni Sutherland and Sheen. Though the film made over $50 million, it was a disappointment. It seemed as though all involved in the film were quite happy to collect a big paycheck for going through the motions and getting to hang out in Europe.

****

Back in Hollywood, Sutherland promptly notched his second DUI arrest. This time the judge wasn't as lenient. Faced with a choice of twelve days in jail or 211 hours of community service, he chose to avoid jail.

****

As a favor to Lou Diamond Phillips, Sutherland's next film appearance was in a very brief, uncredited cameo as a roadblock cop in a movie called *Teresa's Tattoo*. The movie is a pure example of a vanity project. It is the tale of a meek mathematician who is taken out partying by friends during college spring break and ends up kidnapped, drugged, tattooed, and decked out in skin-tight leather clothes. The film was directed by Julie Cypher, whose main claim to fame today is being the mother of two children with former same-sex partner Melissa Etheridge, who also makes a cameo in the film as a hooker. *Young Guns* stars Phillips and Casey Siemaszko were among the male leads.

The lack of good material coming his way and his anchorless personal life had Sutherland looking for something he could sink himself into. The next role he took gave him something he could be passionate enough about to leave Hollywood for a while to pursue. The film was *The Cowboy Way*; the something was rodeo.

The Cowboy Way is hardly a great movie. It tells the story of two buddies, Sonny and Pepper, who are professional rodeo riders. When their Hispanic pal, Nacho Salazar, goes missing in New York City, where he had gone to pick up his daughter, the two friends decide to head east to find him. But these two cowboys from New

Mexico know nothing about life in the big city, and they fall into all kinds of misadventures. With the help of a New York cop, Pepper and Sonny find out that Nacho has been killed, and his daughter, Teresa, has been kidnapped for the underground slave trade. Pepper and Sonny decide to rescue her—the cowboy way.

The movie is a standard fish-out-of-water adventure story, but what makes this film at least watchable are the terrific performances by Sutherland as Sonny Gilstrap and Woody Harrelson as Pepper Lewis. Just about every review of the movie waved it off as a minor diversion that featured good work by the two leads. *Rolling Stone*'s Peter Travers praised Sutherland's quiet intensity while noting that Woody Harrelson was clearly enjoying the hell out of playing his role, originally written for Kevin Costner. The film's bad guy, the crime boss, was ridiculously overplayed by Dylan McDermott, and the cynical but sympathetic New York City cop was played well by the always reliable Ernie Hudson.

The Cowboy Way was released in the early summer of 1994 and brought in just over $20 million at the box office, which was much lower than expected. "I thought it was a fun idea when I first read it," says Sutherland. "I wanted to play a rodeo rider. I got right into it; I spent literally all my off time practicing my roping technique. I would sit in my hotel suite and rope everything in sight until I got very good at it."

A story came out at the time that he was so intent on improving his roping skills that he would lasso everything he could on the set as well. One day as a young female production assistant was walking from one part of the set to another, Sutherland, hidden behind a telephone pole with his rope, lassoed her perfectly. The rope slipped over her head and shoulders, down past her hips and around her ankles. Sutherland then yanked sharply on the rope to tighten the noose, but he did it too hard, pulling the girl off balance and dropping her heavily to the ground. Though not hurt, the young woman was upset and a bit shaken. "I felt horrible about that part," Sutherland later said of the incident.

Perhaps the title was prophetic—after *The Cowboy Way* was finished, Sutherland made a decision. Through his film career he had discovered new passions, one for horses, another for roping. So, a bit like Mickey Rourke walking away from movies to become a professional boxer, Sutherland took a break from his career and became a professional rodeo rider.

RIDING AND ROPING

"I was driving all over the country, and it was a lot of fun. I felt like a tough guy."

–Kiefer Sutherland

Sutherland was a product of the union of two very talented actors and had adopted their profession almost inevitably, as if it were in his blood. His life played out on stages and movie sets, and even in the tabloids. His soul was fueled by the people on the streets, for he needed people around; he was a performer and he needed an audience. Yet when he started making films in the open and often silent spaces of the American West, he discovered a very different part of himself. He discovered a passion for horses. It wasn't just because he got to play cowboy in a couple of films; even his stint in a European-style horse opera reinforced the feeling. The way he tells it: "*Young Guns* was where I began to love horses, but it was when we were shooting *The Three Musketeers* in Europe that my love of riding really took hold. It was there that I got really good on horseback."

Sutherland went so far as to purchase the horses he rode in *Young Guns* and *Young Guns II* and installed them on an 818-acre spread he bought in the Santa Ynez Valley, about three hours northwest of Los Angeles. He made it a working ranch, outfitting it with livestock and equipment and spent much of his time there. When he wasn't working, he was riding and caring for his horses. He wasn't merely playing cowboy anymore.

* * * *

American actors—and despite being UK born and a Canadian citizen, Sutherland is very much an American actor—have a complex relationship with cowboys. The cowboy used to be one of the permanent icons of American cinema. Once, the qualities that made a man were typified by the cowboy than in any other character type in cinema. A loner, the cowboy embodied the American ideals of moral strength and physical heroism, courage, and stoicism. Gary Cooper personified this best in films like *The Virginian, The Plainsman,* and *High Noon.*

Later came others, the *noir* detective especially. These were derivative icons, updated cowboys, but they shared the same essence, and the few actors who were able to project these qualities convincingly became icons themselves. Humphrey Bogart, a New Yorker, almost never appeared on a horse, but his characters in *The Maltese Falcon* and *Casablanca* were cut from the same cloth. John Wayne hated horses, but John Ford made him an iconic cowboy anyway. Many others strapped on six guns but merely portrayed the fantasy; very few actors have embodied the real thing.

The heyday of the Western now is over. Clint Eastwood's *Unforgiven* may be the last cowboy movie, and Eastwood himself may be the last believable film cowboy. But these values remain close to the American soul; people still respond to the qualities that made the cowboy iconic. The question now is only what form will they take: What icon will replace the cowboy? And who will embody it?

* * * *

At the end of 1993, Sutherland was trying his hand at playing a modern cowboy in *The Cowboy Way*. In the film, his character is a rodeo rider, steer roper. Sutherland was a good rider and felt that, with a little coaching, he would be able to play the part convincingly. But to lend authenticity to the film, he would need a double to do the things that he wasn't capable of doing. That man was John English, a real cowboy from New Mexico.

"I had moved with my family to California," English says. "And one thing that cowboys do out there for a bit of side work is they do movie and TV stunt work or doubling work. I was introduced to some movie people and that led to me being hired on as Kiefer's double on *The Cowboy Way*."

"We hit it off right away," English recalls. "We were on the set together a lot and in wardrobe a lot because we wore the same things. He was constantly asking me about life on the circuit. He would say often, 'I would love to try that,' or 'That's something I have got to try.' I thought he was just caught up in the whole excitement of making the movie, but turns out he wasn't."

After the shoot, Sutherland asked English if he would come work on Sutherland's Santa Ynez ranch, and the two eventually talked about putting a team together to enter some USTRC [U.S. Team Roping Championships, the national organizing body of the sport] events. "I made sure Kiefer knew going in that this was not a sport you just dabbled in," English emphasizes. "Roping isn't like picking up a bag of golf clubs. It's an expensive sport, and that expense is what actually forces some good cowboys out of it. The expense wasn't a particular problem with Kiefer, but despite what folks think, even movie stars like Kiefer Sutherland don't have an endless supply of money."

Team roping is also demanding of a person's skill. But on this level, English was satisfied with Sutherland's efforts: "He was as dedicated to practicing and taking this seriously as anyone I have ever seen in the sport. Even when he was off working on a film, if we had an event coming up, I would call Kiefer and tell him we needed to do some practicing. No matter what, every time, he would come up to the ranch and do whatever we needed to do to prepare for the event."

Team roping is a race against time. A steer is released from a chute, and after it has gone a set distance, the riders start after it. Then first roper, the "header' must lasso the steer round the neck in one of three ways: around the neck, around the neck and over one horn, or around both horns. Once the header has secured the steer in what is called a legal catch, he must quickly wrap the rope around his saddle horn a few times and maneuver his horse to tighten the rope and line up the steer so his partner, the "heeler," has a clear shot at lassoing the steer's hind legs. "This is the tough part," English emphasizes. "Once you've made the catch, getting the steer turned around and the rope tightened up, all while you are on the fly, takes a lot of precision and instinct."

The heeler must lasso the steer around both hind legs—he will be penalized five seconds, a huge amount in this event, if he only catches the steer by one leg—so the ability to be able to get the rope around both legs on the first throw is crucial. The heeler then has to quickly make the rope taut by wrapping it around the horn of his saddle a few times and easing his horse backward. Time is called when both riders' ropes are taut and the steer is immobilized. It was hurrying to get the rope wrapped around his saddle horn that caused Sutherland to break every single one of his fingers at least once.

Once both catches are made the header and heeler back up their horses a bit to stretch out the steer and immobilize it. Once that is done the official waves a flag to stop the clock. "At a small, well-kept arena, a good team can get that done in five or six seconds," explains English. "If you're in a bigger space it might take you twice that. So a good time is established at the event; there is no real constant perfect time."

Kiefer was always the header. "He was good. He could ride very well and he could rope," says English. "You cannot compete at that level if you're just going through the motions; you have to know what you're doing." English attributes some of that skill to Sutherland's profession. "You know, I think the fact that he was an actor, a professional actor, for a long time before we did the circuit together actually helped him in his roping. Actors are mimics, they observe people and situations and are able to absorb what they are observing to build characters and performances. That power of observation gave Kiefer an advantage over a lot of rookies, because he could see what they were doing wrong and what they were doing right and file it away."

Sutherland and English won their very first major outing. "We picked up a buckle at that first event we entered, in Arizona," English remembers (Along with prize money, rodeo winners receive an ornate belt buckle as a trophy). "We had ridden in a couple other events, but this was the first USTRC-sanctioned event that we went in, and we did real well."

"I was as shocked as anyone when we won that first rodeo," says Sutherland. "But I'm a very competitive person, and I wanted that buckle." That first win had its price, though, according to English: "Kiefer got beaten up pretty good, broke a few fingers. But those are injuries that happen in roping. Worse even, many guys have had their thumbs mangled so bad they have to be amputated. These are the hazards of steer roping."

Sutherland has said in passing that he "broke every bone in his body" while roping, and though this is an obvious exaggeration, English makes it plain that Sutherland wasn't spared his fair share of injuries. "Kiefer's a tough dude, and he was banged up a lot. He did break every finger on each hand; he had a knee cap shattered on him. He had shoulder injuries, wrist injuries. But he bounced back. A lot of times he tried to keep the injuries to himself so not to make a big deal out of them. There were times after an event, even if it was just a little jackpot event, he would give it a hundred and fifty percent. The next day when we'd be packing up to head out I could see he was hurting bad, and he would mention it in passing. But he never made a thing out of it, he just got on with it. I think that was all part of his reason for being out there. Everything that happens out there once the gate swings open is real; what you feel is real, the knocks and that adrenaline rush for doing it right as well. I think Kiefer was looking for that, looking to connect with things that were stark and real."

After that initial success, Sutherland, English, and their team spent most of summer 1994 driving around the western United States competing in rodeos. They only won one more time that first year, in Albuquerque, New Mexico, but they all had fun. "I quit school when I was sixteen," Sutherland says. "I missed that socialization. I missed just being a guy and hanging around with other guys. I missed out on learning about life by experiencing it for real instead of learning about life by researching movie roles. So there I was all of a sudden at twenty-five years old traveling around the country with a few funny guys and three horses. Those were my college years. It was fantastic."

There is an oft-repeated story that Sutherland and English won a U.S. national team-roping championship: "I have read a lot of that stuff too," English says. "But you've never heard either Kiefer or I say such. Kiefer and I won a few buckles in Scottsdale, Arizona, and in New Mexico. He also won lots of little events riding with other guys that I paired him with. "

Despite being a novice, Sutherland had some talent for the event. "He was really good on a horse. I knew that from the film we worked on together. He loves horses and knows how to ride and care for them, so I would have to say that that was his biggest asset. Horsemanship is the probably the main thing a competitor needs to be good at this sport, and one aspect of good horsemanship is connecting with a good horse. You generally work with just one when you are training at first, so the horse gets to know the routine and gets set in the pattern, then you only have to concentrate on the roping; the horse will do his job without much prompting."

The team traveled with a number of horses because, as English explained, "After a person gets to roping well, they usually need a practice horse to ride so they can run more steers and save their number-one horse for the competitions." Sutherland's first main horse was named Till; he later had two others, Guthrie and Bucky.

Sutherland also worked hard to bring his roping up to standard. "He could rope too; you can't compete at this level if you can't rope," English emphasizes. "He would practice that constantly, even when we were waiting around, he would be practicing.

As much as Sutherland enjoyed rodeo riding and his own team, he still had to pay his dues. "For the first year, the rest of the guys on the circuit—the hardcore cowboys—kind of made fun of me. But then they saw that I wasn't backing down from the criticism, and after a while they stopped seeing me as a movie actor and saw that I could really rope." Sutherland doesn't neglect to give credit where credit is due, either. "I wasn't a natural cowboy, or a natural roper, but what I lacked there I made up for in my horses," he says. "Roping is one of those sports like polo, where the better your horse is, the better you are. I had some great horses."

Life on the road for rodeo cowboys is worlds away from the comfort and luxury that even a B-movie actor can afford. For a steer-roping team even on the big USTRC circuit there is lots of driving, lots of long highways, and lots of motels. During those long hours on the open road between rodeo events, the team had plenty of time for conversation. "Kiefer was much more interested in talking about our world. It was now his world, but he was still a bit of a stranger to it," English remembers. "He was very open to talking about anything we wanted to talk about. He said a lot of negative things about the Hollywood system, about how everyone was out to step on and over anyone else and how people would lie and cheat as a part of the daily routine of getting ahead. He said he liked the roping world because everyone was fair. We all loved what we were doing. We all cheered for the other guy to do his best and wished for the best team to come out on top. I remember him talking an awful lot about his daughter, too. He is so proud of her."

Sutherland was low man on the totem pole in terms of experience and accepted the low-end duties without complaint. He had to feed, water, and clean up after the horses, and take care of their gear. This impressed English: "The thing about Kiefer that I remember from those days is that he never complained about anything. He worked as hard as anyone I've ever seen. It was almost like he was over compensating, maybe because he thought everyone in our world would be thinking less of him because of who he was in his world."

Sutherland also seems to have put his wilder side on hold. "Sure, after events we would have some fun and blow off some steam," English says. "But when we were on the road, going from one event to another, it was hard work. It requires that everyone on the team be on the ball. You can't win steer-roping events if you are drunk or hung over—it is a professional sport."

To the other cowboys, Sutherland was not special. As Jeff Sanders, who has won his fair share of USTRC team-roping events, tells it, "What you have to remember is that these events are top-to-bottom filled with all different kinds of characters. You have millionaire CEOs out there competing to prove to themselves that they are real men, and you have your hardcore cowboys who really need the check they're competing for, because if they don't win it they don't have gas money to get home. With that kind of mix out there, most folks who acknowledged him at all would say something like, 'Oh yeah, that guy there is Kiefer Sutherland the movie actor.' But it would always be followed by, 'So, can he rope?' Because that is what it all comes down to out there; who or what you are outside the event means nothing to nobody. That goes for Kiefer and it goes for me and it goes for every roper out there."

Sanders continues, "I remember seeing Kiefer around. There was never any look-at-me-I'm-a-movie-star swagger on him. He took it serious. I saw him compete just a couple of times and competed against him once, in Arizona I believe, and he was pretty good at it; he could get it done. But again, he was just one of hundreds of guys and women out there doing it. Your event is called, your name is called, your partner's name is called, the gates open and you do it.

Then you dust yourself off, and the next guys' names are called."

John English agrees that the name Kiefer Sutherland was nothing special to the real cowboys, "No, they really didn't care who he was. They generally only care about whether or not the guy can ride and rope, and Kiefer could ride and rope."

And unlike most stars, while he was out among the rodeo riders, Sutherland was entirely approachable. "Kiefer would never turn anyone away, ever," English points out. "If someone wanted to come up and talk to him about roping or the event, he would talk to them. If they wanted to talk to him about one of his movies, he would gladly talk to them about that too. He really wanted to just fit in there and do his best and earn his applause."

And the reverse was also true. Sutherland would often keep to himself to observe and learn, but when he wanted to congratulate another cowboy on a great ride or ask about a piece of equipment he was using, he would do it respectfully. "The other guys on the circuit never paid much attention to him at all," says English. "Well, let me put it this way: they noticed him as much as they would notice anyone else there to rope. All they cared about is if he could rope and then they cared about beating our time. That's it. But because he worked hard and was respectful of every other cowboy, he was pretty well liked out there."

During their time on the road together, Sutherland and the team earned three buckles for winning events, and they also placed in a number of events and earned a bit of money in each.

* * * *

Rodeo has the image of being a brutal sport. In some ways it is, though not in the way many people think. Both English and

Sanders, both long-time veterans of the sport, say they have never seen a steer badly injured during an event. "The ropes around their necks and legs detach very quickly and easily once the run is finished," English explains. "I have, however, seen many guys badly injured during the events." Indeed, the sport is far harder on the human competitors than on the animals they are roping or riding. Sanders once saw a female competitor lose a finger when it got caught between the rope and her saddle horn. Broken bones are commonplace in virtually all the events, and anyone who has seen a Brahma bull go after a rider it has just bucked off appreciates the inherent frailty of men in the face of nature.

If you are not tough, you do not survive long in rodeo. It requires not the work-out-with-your-personal-trainer kind of tough, but one that comes from being able to function while in pain. This kind of tough means knowing that when you go to bed, you're going to hurt even more in the morning. Pain is the rite of passage in the cowboy world. Sutherland paid his dues in skills learned, injuries suffered and competitions won. He earned the respect of the cowboys he was competing with and against, and by the time he stopped competing, Kiefer Sutherland was one of them.

* * * *

Sutherland competed in team roping over a period of five years. As English clarifies, "We actually were doing roping events together from those early days in '94 through about '99. But Kiefer was not with us the whole time; he was often off somewhere making movies. We traveled around together for maybe six, eight months if you add it all up. But that was spread over five years. He was working steady in movies, sometimes way out of the country. But we would keep in touch, and when I told him he ought to meet up with us for an event, more often than not he would be there and he would be ready."

After winning a big USTRC event in Scottsdale in 1998, Sutherland and the team entered a few more events, but they stopped competing in 1999. There were a couple of reasons for this, according to English. "It's an expensive sport to maintain a current status in, and Kiefer was getting busier and busier. He told me once, near the time we stopped competing, that he realized his life as a movie actor was a privilege. He took it for granted for a long time, and just like he had felt it was time to take a break, he felt that it was now time to get back in that game. Then not long after that he started doing *24*, and he had even less time."

"Every once in a while, I'll get a call from Kiefer," says English. "He wants to talk about how things are going, what's happening with the other guys. Likewise, I'll give him a call if I'm thinking about him, wondering how he is doing. You get quite close to a guy when you travel the circuit, and that doesn't stop just because the competitions stop." Asked whether there was the chance they would compete again, he laughs, "Well, steer roping isn't a sport you just jump in and out of. But I'll tell you, once that sport is in you, it stays in you. Just because neither of us will ever probably compete in a rodeo event again doesn't mean we don't think about it a lot."

When Sutherland stopped competing and decided to re-focus on his acting career, he moved back to Los Angeles full time. In January 2000, he sold his Santa Ynez ranch for about $3.6 million and stopped being a cowboy except in films.

* * * *

Asked why Sutherland took up roping in the first place, English pauses for a few moments before responding: "We did talk about stuff like that; we spent a lot of time together on the road and at events. He was at a kind of delicate place in his life at the time. He was working in movies and making good money, but he wasn't doing work that he thought was any good, and he was feeling everything he had worked for slipping away. He was also having some personal issues, too, family stuff. Roping gave him something he could concentrate on, something he could focus on away from Hollywood. And he told me that it was through that experience, through our roping, that he found his way back to the work that he does best, acting."

12

KELLY

"There was a point when I either wasn't being offered anything at all or what I was getting were exact copies of my previous work. Or they were simply not very good projects at all. I didn't feel I had the kind of energy that was needed to go out and pursue projects. I guess you could say I was burned out."

–Kiefer Sutherland

After *The Cowboy Way,* Sutherland's movie career seemed to be on the skids. It was the only film he released in 1994, and he released nothing in 1995. The quality of the projects he was being offered was getting worse, and the quality of his own work was going down, too. One good project that came Sutherland's way during this time involved a second stint behind the camera for a television job, this time for an episode of *Fallen Angels,* an Emmy-winning anthology series that ran on the Showtime cable network for two seasons, from 1993 to 1995. The show used the hard-boiled crime fiction of such masters as Raymond Chandler, Dashiell Hammett, and Jim Thompson as the basis for weekly mini film noir movies.

Fallen Angels was produced by Mirage Enterprises, whose founder, the late and great filmmaker Sydney Pollack, was executive producer. Throughout his career, Pollack was a quiet champion of young talent, and he used this series as a showcase for many first-time filmmakers. The second episode of the first season, *I'll Be Waiting,* based on the 1939 Raymond Chandler short story, was directed by Tom Hanks. Tom Cruise directed the fifth episode of that season, a film version of Jim Thompson's story *The Frightening Frammis.*

Sutherland was chosen to direct the first episode of the second season, *Love and Blood.* This episode was taken from a story by Evan Hunter about a boxer's wife who at first leaves her husband for another man, but then has a change of heart. She decides she loves her husband and wants to give the marriage another chance. So she returns to him just as he is being framed for a murder he did not commit.

Sutherland not only directed this episode, he also played Matt Cordell, the boxer. His wife was played by Mädchen Amick, of *Twin Peaks* fame. He rounded out his cast with two actors who were themselves ex-cons before making good, Edward Bunker and Danny Trejo. Once again Sutherland showed an assurance behind the camera. He infused the film with mood and style but let the actors and the story drive the action.

After filming, Sutherland went back out to finish 1994 on the rodeo circuit with John English, and in early 1995 was offered a part in a no-frills thriller entitled *Freeway*. The low-budget movie—it cost a miniscule $3 million—was written and directed by Matthew Bright, whose nightmarish, post-modern screenplay was based on the children's fable "Little Red Riding Hood."

In the story, a teenage runaway called Vanessa, played by a young Reese Witherspoon, has escaped the clutches of her social worker and is headed to her grandmother's house. She is followed and taunted by a charismatic man named Bob Wolverton, played by Sutherland. The man turns out to be a pedophile and a serial killer. This was the baddest of the bad guys Sutherland had played, and he had great fun doing it. He alternates an angelic smile with a diabolic grimace and smooth speech with snarling. His performance is so good that it is hard to imagine anyone else playing it.

Freeway is a very creepy movie; it is haunting, profane, and violent. While it is a stylish, well crafted piece of filmmaking, it is a very uncomfortable movie to watch. Most of the characters are morally repugnant, including Vanessa's own parents: her mother is a hooker and her father, a drug addict. Roger Ebert wrote in his review of the film, "Like it or hate it—or both—you have to admire its skill and the over-the-top virtuosity of Kiefer Sutherland and Reese Witherspoon as the wolf and the little girl."

Released in January 1996, *Freeway* played film festivals around the world, starting with a very popular splash at Sundance. The film did not do well at the box office when it was released to American theaters, probably because of its content, although it later became a major home-video cult hit.

For of the rest of 1995, Sutherland's acting career was in a slump. Some might argue that during this time he was doing some of his most interesting work to date, but if so, there wasn't a lot of it. His sense of discontentment and of being directionless remained. Reflecting upon this period, he says, "I have had some great career highs, but my lows were very, very low. All of a sudden, I started to appreciate the fantastic opportunities that I had been taking for granted."

* * * *

In mid-1995, Sutherland met fellow Canadian Kelly Winn: tall, blue-eyed, and six years his senior. The two quickly became inseparable and, after eight months of dating, were married in a quiet ceremony on June 29, 1996. When he and Winn decided to marry, they chose to have the ceremony at St. Andrew's College, the boarding school that he had attended when he was twelve.

Sutherland was very much in love with Winn and wanted the marriage to work. "The first time I got married my intentions were sincere, but I was really getting married for all the wrong reasons," he says now. "This second time around, I wanted to prove to myself that I had learned from that first experience, and I went into my marriage to Kelly bursting with enthusiasm and commitment."

But old habits die hard. Not long after their marriage, the couple was playing pool and drinking with Sutherland's half-brother Roeg at a bar in downtown Toronto. The booze had been flowing liberally for hours. Then one of the men they were playing pool with, who had also been drinking, began flirting with Kelly, unaware that she was Kiefer's wife. At first, Kiefer didn't seem to care. But when the man actually bent down and licked Kelly's foot, it got Sutherland's attention. He told the guy that it was fine to want to have a good time, but that the man had just touched his wife inappropriately. Sutherland twice asked the guy to apologize. "She asked me to do it," the guy responded. Sutherland went berserk. "I hit him hard, and he went down," he remembers. The actor continued to punch and kick the man so savagely that by the time Roeg Sutherland pulled him off, an ambulance needed to be called. The pool table they had been playing on was destroyed. Sutherland paid for the damages, and luckily no one called the authorities, because he almost certainly would have been hauled away from the place in handcuffs.

Sutherland later commented on the incident: "I remember crying late that night, and I don't cry a lot. I cried over why I did that to this guy. I've got over 180 stitches in my head from fights where I have gotten my ass kicked, and I've never felt bad about that. But when I win a fight, I always feel the other person didn't deserve what he got."

****

While it is probably an exaggeration to say that Sutherland was being typecast as a villain, some of his best roles were bad guys. Producer Bernie Goldmann puts it this way: "Kiefer's a scary guy. He has such intensity. He can convey a sense of menace without raising his voice or raising his hand, and he seems so much more physically threatening on screen than he is in reality. I believe it comes through his eyes and the way he holds his body, the way he moves. He can just look at you and you want to back away. Then, you hang out with him after a scene, and he goes back to being the sweetest, nicest guy in the world, so you know he has a real gift." Sutherland himself is more circumspect about this aspect of his talent: "I like playing bad guys. But after a while there is only so much you can do with a sneer or menacing look."

Nevertheless, in the three major movies he made from 1995 to 1996, he played the heavy. He got second billing in *Eye for an Eye,* another big-studio project for Paramount Pictures. Based on the tautly written novel by Erika Holzer, *Eye for an Eye* concerns a woman named Karen McCann (Sally Field), whose daughter is brutally raped and murdered. McCann tries hard to bring the killer, Robert Doob (Sutherland), to justice. To the horror of McCann and the detective working on the case (Joe Mantegna), Doob is released on a technicality. Doob harasses McCann, telling her that he will come after her youngest daughter if she does not stop pushing his case. Getting little help from the support groups she has been going to, the frightened and angry mother joins a gun club to learn how to shoot. Then Doob rapes and kills another woman and is again released from prison on a technicality. At this point, McCann decides to take matters into her own hands so that the psychopath will not kill again.

When *Eye for an Eye* was released in January 1996, it was met with negative reviews. Roger Ebert described it as manipulative and trashy and declared, "Movies like this cheapen our character." Sutherland fared a bit better, but even supporters like *Rolling Stone*'s Peter Travers called Sutherland's performance one dimensional. They were now asking themselves what had happened to the mercurial but talented young actor who used to take such command of the screen.

On the home front, Sutherland was enjoying his new wife and extended family. Kelly Winn brought Kiefer two stepsons, Julian, age six, and Timothy, age three, whom Sutherland grew close to almost immediately. And while there was no indication of a complete change in his ways, he was giving this marriage a lot more effort and concentration than he did his first. Sutherland was still heading off occasionally to do rodeo competitions, but as 1995 ended and his relationship with Winn deepened, he became more settled. He had a family to take care of and needed regular work.

To fill the unaccustomed gaps in his schedule, he started doing smaller projects. One of the first was an uncredited walk-on, again with Lou Diamond Phillips, in *Hourglass*, a film written and directed by, as well as starring, their good friend C. Thomas Howell. From the walk-on, Sutherland went to an ensemble effort, *Duke of Groove*, which ended up being nominated for the Academy Award for best live-action short film of 1995. *Duke of Groove* was written and directed by the talented actor and filmmaker Griffin Dunne. It tells a very poignant story about a mother, played by Kate Capshaw, who takes her son to a wild party so he will not be home when his father leaves for the last time. At the party, mother and son mingle with pop celebrities and learn something about themselves in the process. For once Sutherland plays a decent character; he is the suave host of the party, identified in the credits only as "The Host." Elliot Gould is also in the film, as are Uma Thurman, Tobey Maguire, and Carey Lowell.

* * * *

The Lost Boys director Joel Schumacher says that he has thought about Kiefer Sutherland for at least one of the roles in just about every film he has done. "Kiefer is thought of as a wild man, and he is to a large extent," he says. "But the Kiefer I have known and worked with so often has never been late to set once, has never been unruly or unprofessional. So that is what I base my opinion on, not what I read in tabloids." Schumacher called Kiefer again in 1996 for a small but pivotal role in the big-budget film adaptation of John Grisham's novel *A Time to Kill*. This film also marked just the second occasion that Donald and Kiefer Sutherland appeared in the same film, although they did not share any scenes together.

A Time to Kill tells the story of a black man in Mississippi whose young daughter is brutally raped by a couple of rednecks. The rapists are arrested, but the father of the girl, Carl Lee Hailey (Samuel L. Jackson), believes that the racist judicial system in Mississippi will let them walk free. He waits for the rapists at the courthouse with an assault rifle and kills them both. Charged with murder, he hires young lawyer Jake Brigance (Matthew McConaughey) to defend him, and his case becomes a *cause célèbre* within the legal community. Racial tensions rise when the brother of one of the murdered rapists, Sutherland's Freddie Lee Cobb, convinces the local Ku Klux Klan to take up his cause against Hailey.

The film is quite provocative, appearing to condone murder if the circumstances warrant it. It was his distaste for this message that led Paul Newman to turn down the role of Lucien Wilbanks, the old liberal lawyer who advises Brigance. Donald Sutherland was cast in the role instead. As is the case with many big-studio package projects, Schumacher had to go through several other casting changes, with John Grisham himself holding final say over who would play which character.

Schumacher had originally cast Matthew McConaughey in the role of Freddie Lee Cobb, the role that Kiefer Sutherland ended up playing. But McConaughey was convinced that he could play Brigance, the lead. The role had already been turned down by Val Kilmer, the star of *Batman Forever*, which Schumacher had just finished directing. Woody Harrelson and Kevin Costner also expressed interest in the role, but John Grisham had vetoed them. So when McConaughey came to him, Schumacher was all ears. He gave McConaughey a private audition and promptly agreed to cast him as Brigance. This would be McConaughey's big break. But having McConaughey as Brigance meant that Schumacher had nobody for Freddie Lee Cobb. That was when he turned to Sutherland, who immediately accepted. "I have a good relationship with Joel," Sutherland says. "When he asks me to do a movie with him, I will do it if I am available." And at this point in time, Sutherland happened to be available a lot.

A Time to Kill did a brisk business on its opening weekend in July 1996, but it turned out to be barely profitable. It only earned $49 million domestically, while it cost $40 million to make. The reviews were mixed, with most critics declaring the 148-minute film much too long. And while Donald Sutherland got consistently positive notices, his son Kiefer again received negative reviews for playing his character as a cliché-riddled racist. Given the limitations of Akiva Goldsman's screenplay, however, it is clear that there wasn't much depth he could have brought to Cobb on his own.

While *A Time to Kill* made a movie star out of Matthew McConaughey, for Kiefer Sutherland it was just another bad-guy role and a paycheck. His performance did nothing to revive his career, and his slump continued to deepen.

13

DIRECT TO VIDEO

"I never stopped working. Granted, a lot of the stuff I was doing was substandard, but I never quit working. It all started to feel a bit pointless."

–Kiefer Sutherland

In 1996 and 1997, Sutherland's career continued down a slow but steady path to obscurity. His offers were limited, but he tried nonetheless to accept only the best of them. He was still young, only thirty-three. He played primarily low-lives, losers, criminals—people a bit like himself in a way, down-and-out and on the receiving end of life. Sutherland wouldn't let up, however. He always tried to exercise some sort of selectivity; he varied the mix, acting here, directing there. What else could he do?

* * * *

Scottish actor Dayton Callie, who had been around forever, most recently in the Rob Zombie horror movie *Halloween II* and the TV series *Sons of Anarchy*, decided in 1996 that the best way to get interesting acting roles was to simply write them himself. Sylvester Stallone had done this successfully two decades earlier with *Rocky*. So Callie wrote two scripts: *Executive Target*, which starred Michael Madsen and Roy Scheider; and *The Last Days of Frankie the Fly*. Callie himself appeared in both films, although he only received fifth billing in each.

The Last Days of Frankie the Fly, like other films in the post-*Reservoir Dogs/Pulp Fiction* era, is a crime drama with quirky dialogue, over-the-top violence, and characters that border on the surreal. Frankie is a small-time hood in Los Angeles who works for a mob boss named Sal. Frankie falls in love with a young porn actress named Margaret, who desperately wants to be a legitimate star. Sal considers her to be his property and wants to keep her where she is, but the smitten Frankie decides to stand up to Sal to try to save Margaret from her squalid situation.

What makes this film more than just a curiosity is the casting. Dennis Hopper stars, somewhat against type, as the dumped-upon Frankie and delivers a performance full of idiosyncratic gems. Daryl Hannah plays Margaret with a sweet sincerity that seems completely out of place with her sleazy Los Angeles surroundings. Michael Madsen, with his hulking form, squinty eyes, and gravelly voice, is totally convincing as a mob boss.

Sutherland's role in *Frankie the Fly* is one of the most interesting things he did during this low period. Instead of a criminal, for once, he plays Joey, a pretentious NYU Film School grad who goes to Hollywood to become another Martin Scorsese, only to wind up directing Margaret's porn films. Whatever strengths the film may have had, however, it never saw the inside of an American theater and only appeared in video here in late 1997. This, alas, was the basic pattern for Sutherland's films during these years.

****

Another Tarantino-esque writer trying to make a name for himself at the time was Brad Mirman. In 1996, he was shopping around a screenplay called *Truth or Consequences, N.M.*, which found its way into Sutherland's hands. The actor was interested in the lead character of Curtis Freley, another well-spoken criminal. Sutherland was still a big enough name to get a low-budget movie produced, and he was able to get Triumph Films to back the project. On the strength of his earlier directorial successes on television, Sutherland was approved to direct the film, his first aimed for theatrical release. Good actors were more than happy to be involved with Sutherland on the film, and Vincent Gallo and Mykelti Williamson were cast as his co-leads. Even actors Rod Steiger and Martin Sheen were game to fill a couple of small roles.

Released in May 1997, *Truth or Consequences, N.M.* is a standard drug-deal-gone-bad story with a few twists. Raymond Lembecke, Gallo's character, wants revenge on Tony Vago (Rod Steiger), a crime boss who set him up for prison. To get even, Lembecke plans to steal a million dollars' worth of drugs from Vago. Teaming with fellow criminal Marcus Weans (Williamson) and disturbed killer Curtis Freley (Sutherland), they make the heist and flee towards Las Vegas. On the way they kidnap a couple in an RV. The male hostage starts to enjoy the adventure and wants to join the thieves. They are stalked all the while by Martin Sheen, as the drug boss's assassin.

To Sutherland's credit, he refuses to depict criminal psychopaths as cool and clever rebels, à la Tarantino, when in fact they are usually sad, pathetic losers. His Curtis Freley is a vicious, paranoid character, more animal than human. Vincent Gallo came away with a high opinion of Sutherland, feeling he was one of the more confident actor-directors he had worked with. "I've done it myself, that's how I know," Gallo says. "It's hard to concentrate on playing a character consistently while you're worrying about everything else that goes on during a shoot. Kiefer's a smart guy, very smart. He was able to compartmentalize everything." Martin Sheen also enjoyed working with the young director: "I knew Kiefer through my son Emilio Estevez; I had just done *The War at Home* with [Emilio] directing. I kind of enjoyed feeding off their youthful energy."

Sadly, *Truth or Consequences, N.M.* appeared in only seven theaters, bringing in a total of just $109,261. It went to video in a matter of weeks.

* * * *

Sutherland continued to use his voice to fill gaps in his schedule and in his income by doing voice-over work for commercials, narrated documentaries, and in animated films. Among these efforts was dubbing the male lead for the English version of the 1997 Japanese anime film *Armitage III: Poly-Matrix*.

He took another detour in his career in the late spring of 1997. He made a rare appearance on the stage, starring alongside his mother, Shirley Douglas, in Tennessee Williams's *The Glass Menagerie* at the Royal Alexandra Theatre in downtown Toronto.

The Glass Menagerie was Williams's first successful play, and by all accounts it is the closest thing to a purely autobiographical piece that he ever wrote. It is told from the perspective of Tom Wingfield, played by Sutherland, who looks back at his relationship with his overbearing mother Amanda and his sad, introverted sister Laura, who spends all her time with her collection of glass figurines. Tom

Photo byDPA/ZUMA Press/KEYSTONE Press

Kiefer Sutherland in March 2009, at the German premiere of *Monsters and Aliens*.

Time & Life Pictures/Getty Images

The Sutherland family, May 1970. From left: Kiefer, father Donald, stepbrother Thomas, sister Rachel, and mother Shirley Douglas.

© Warner Brothers/ZUMA Press/KEYSTONE Press

Donald Sutherland in *Start the Revolution Without Me* (1970).

Kiefer Sutherland and wife Kelly Winn in 1999.

HRC/Wenn.com/KEYSTONE Press

Donald Sutherland and Shirley Douglas.

Getty Images / Frank Edwards/Contributor

Grant/FOTOS Int'l/KEYSTONE Press

Kiefer Sutherland with fiancée Julia Roberts at the 1991 Academy Awards.

©Fotos Int'l/Keystone Press

Kiefer and Donald Sutherland.

A still from *The Lost Boys* (Sutherland is second from the right).

Photo by Dane Andrew/Zuma Press/KEYSTONE Press

Donald Sutherland.

Getty Images / Donald Weber/Contributor

Kiefer Sutherland and his mother, Shirley Douglas.

The cast of *24* celebrating its 150th episode, January 6, 2008 (left to right: Anne Wersching, Kiefer Sutherland, Howard Gordon, Carlos Bernard, Mary Lynn Rajskub).

Kiefer Sutherland receives his star on the Hollywood Walk of Fame, December 9, 2008.

© Vaughn Youtz /ZUMA Press/KEYSTONE Press

Sutherland holds a vintage Gibson guitar.

works in a warehouse and does his best to support them all while his mother and sister act out lives based almost entirely on fantasy.

Director Neil Munro kept the production faithful to the text, giving Douglas and Sutherland the space to play their characters fully; in a remarkable performance, mother and son acted out a relationship far removed from their real personalities. Sutherland didn't just capture the quiet desperation of Tom, he infused the role with a gentle heroism as well; even though the man is surrounded by dysfunction, he finds a way to stay above it. Douglas was a towering presence on stage, inhabiting Amanda completely. Her technique and talent gave the character of Amanda such force that her son seemed almost to cower under the weight and power of her personality.

Sutherland could count this among his finest moments as an actor. But after this brief interlude treading the boards, it was back to what had become the uphill slog of the silver screen.

* * * *

Sutherland's next film, the bold and audacious *Dark City,* was a bright moment in this somber period, but it came about through a tragedy. In the early nineties, Sutherland had befriended another young actor on the rise in Hollywood, Brandon Lee. Lee was the son of a Hollywood legend, martial arts superstar Bruce Lee, who died in 1973, when Brandon was just eight years old. As an actor, Brandon was trying to crawl out from under the far-reaching shadow of his brilliant father. He and Sutherland became friends, perhaps because each knew what it was like to have to create an identity independent of a famous father. The two partied together in L.A. and shared a love of music and guitars as well.

In 1993, Lee was making *The Crow,* a film based on an adult-oriented comic book, a medium now known as the graphic novel. Lee had made a few films prior to *The Crow,* such as *Showdown in Little Tokyo* and *Rapid Fire,* but he was still mostly known as the son of Bruce Lee. *The Crow* is the diametric opposite of his previous films. It is the story of a young musician, Eric Draven, played by Lee, who is murdered by thugs and returns from the dead to avenge himself and his girlfriend, who was murdered with him. The film is dark, even creepy, but it has an unmistakable energy about it. Lee knew that this film was his chance, and threw himself into preparation for the role. He grew his hair long and trained his body until it was a powerful, sinewy machine.

Only eight days before filming was to end, however, tragedy struck. To save time, some dummy rounds (real-looking fake bullets) were made by pouring the gunpowder out of real cartridges and then re-inserting the actual bullet; the primer for the main charge, however, was not removed. One such bullet had been loaded into a gun, but the primer had gone off—no one knows how—with sufficient force to dislodge the head of the bullet and leave it in the barrel. Later, when they were shooting the initial death scene in the film, the gun was loaded with blanks and handed to actor Michael Massee, who was playing one of the thugs. In the scene, the thug aims the gun point-blank at Lee's character and shoots. Massee fired as directed. The blank charge, though weaker than in a real bullet, was enough to propel the bullet out of the barrel and into Lee, where it lodged in his spine. Lee collapsed to the ground as he was supposed to, and Australian director Alex Proyas yelled, "Cut!" But Lee didn't get up. An assistant director noticed that Lee was motionless and that blood was pooling on the ground next to him. Lee was rushed to the hospital but died there two hours later of internal bleeding. The date was March 31, 1993.

Sutherland and Proyas met at Brandon Lee's funeral, and a bond was created through their shared loss. Proyas was so distraught at what happened that it was four years before he made his next film, *Dark City,* which he also wrote. The idea for *Dark City* actually came to him during the shooting of *The Crow*. He had been sitting on the North Carolina set watching his crew reconfigure things, moving around building mock-ups. This gave him an idea for a science fiction story about a time and place where certain people could, through telepathy alone, physically alter their surroundings.

When *Dark City* came together, Proyas wanted Sutherland to play the strangest and most challenging role in the film, that of Dr. Daniel P. Schreber. The plot concerns a man named John Murdock (Rufus Sewell) who wakes up in a strange hotel with no memory of who or where he is. A mysterious phone call from Schreber (Sutherland) alerts him that he is being followed by a group of people called the Strangers. Murdoch flees and comes to realize that he is wanted for a series of murders, although he has no memory of committing them. He discovers he has psychokinetic powers that enable him to witness the Strangers changing the city's landscape and manipulating peoples' memories. Murdoch searches to regain his memory and ultimately teams up with a cop who believes in his innocence. Together they track down Schreber who explains that the Strangers are aliens and the whole city is an experiment they are conducting.

Dark City is a dark, deep, and seriously eccentric movie that demands the audience pay close attention. It is so confusing that when Proyas showed his producers at New Line Cinema his first cut of the film, they demanded that he add a voice-over narration to set the stage for viewers. Proyas fought them hard on the matter but was obliged to insert the narration, which was recorded by Sutherland. The actor himself admits that the film confused him: "I never got it, period," he laughs. "I mean, I understood what Alex had in mind, and I knew what role my character played in the whole thing, but some of the notions and the ideas were a bit unsettling. So I simply just trusted Alex and did what he needed me to do."

Dark City was Sutherland's biggest departure yet from what audiences had come to expect from him. It has been suggested that his character was based in part on the white rabbit from *Alice in Wonderland*, but his performance is more reminiscent of the great actor Peter Lorre. Sutherland limps and walks hunched over; his speech is fractured and breathless, his movements jerky and unstable. He is fantastic in the movie.

Dark City was shot in Australia and used a number of the sets left behind by *The Matrix* in order to keep costs under control. While in Australia, Sutherland was once again a fixture in the local bars. In one incident, he got falling-down drunk in a Sydney pub with no wallet or money on him. Apparently he danced in the middle of the bar floor and whirled around simulating martial arts kicks before a table full of fans finally invited him to join them. He ate a plate full of chicken wings, had a couple more drinks, then thanked his new friends profusely before stumbling out.

Dark City was released on February 27, 1998. At a cost of $27 million, it was not a mega-budget film, but it was still expensive for the kind of movie it was. It only broke even during its theatrical release, but, as is the case with many of Sutherland's movies, the film found a cult audience on the home-video market. On July 29, 2008, Warner Bros. Home Video released Proyas's longer, more complex director's cut, which ended up selling very well even ten years after the film's initial theatrical release.

In contrast to the cool reception it received in theaters, the critical response to the film and to Kiefer Sutherland was spectacular.

Peter Stack wrote in the *San Francisco Chronicle,* "It is hypnotic and haunting and to be sure, dark. It is among the most memorable cinematic ventures in recent years. Maybe there is nothing wrong with a movie that is simply sensational to look at." And of Sutherland he wrote, "Sutherland looks like the overseer of a Nazi mental ward. Limping and speaking in a menacing, spitting slur, he looks like a send-up of a wacko shrink . . . But he looks terrific, despite the mugging. Under Proyas's gaze, he's a character who transcends caricature. Looks aren't deceiving here, they're absolutely everything."

Long-time Kiefer Sutherland fan Roger Ebert was completely blown away by the film: "*Dark City* is a great visionary achievement, a film so original and exciting, it stirred my imagination like *Metropolis* and *2001: A Space Odyssey* did." Ebert named the film to his list of the top ten films of 1998.

****

Sutherland was back Down Under almost immediately, this time to New Zealand. *A Soldier's Sweetheart* tells the story of a Vietnam War field-hospital unit led by an unorthodox medic called Rat Kiley (Kiefer Sutherland). In the story, a younger medic, Mark (played by Skeet Ulrich), decides to sneak his girlfriend from home into Vietman and into the camp. Marianne (Georgina Cates) is completely out of place in the male-dominated war zone, but her presence injects an element of humanity into an otherwise dehumanizing environment. Being in the camp has a maturing effect on Marianne, as she encounters the innumerable tragedies of war. The screenplay is based on "Sweetheart of the Song Tra Bong," a short story by the elegant writer and Vietnam veteran Tim O'Brien.

Thanks to O'Brien's poignant realism and to the stylish direction of Thomas Michael Donnelly, the film has an authenticity and resonance that few Vietnam War films achieve.

The film is good, and Sutherland is very good. Despite the superficial similarities with *M*A*S*H,* Sutherland creates in Kiley a character more introspective about the experience of war than his father's Hawkeye. Director Thomas Michael Donnelly praised Sutherland's participation in the film. "I was thrilled to be working with Kiefer," says Donnelly. "I needed someone who looked a bit rough around the edges, someone who looked like they had lived a bit, not just pretended to live."

Originally, *A Soldier's Sweetheart* was produced for the Showtime cable network as a TV movie, but it was a powerful enough piece that Showtime decided to test the waters and show it theatrically in some markets as well. The network also decided to generate some word of mouth ahead of time by entering the movie in a few film festivals. Interviewed at the Toronto International Film Festival, Sutherland discussed the film's similarity to *M*A*S*H*: "I think that the setting in a medical unit near the front lines of a war is where the similarities begin and end really," he said. "*M*A*S*H* was a dark, comedic, almost allegorical look at war, whereas we were depicting the kind of tragedy that war is responsible for beyond the obvious things like death and maiming and the physical destruction of a country. We were depicting the fracturing of psyches and the destruction of a person's humanity."

* * * *

Far from being evidence of a revival in Sutherland's career, *A Soldier's Sweetheart,* despite its own merits, merely heralded in new lows. Sutherland followed it with a minor potboiler that confirmed the worst: he had sunk even further into the depths of cinematic purgatory. The film, *Break Up,* in which he plays a cop investigating a suspicious murder, was clearly something he only did to keep money rolling in. He followed it with *Ground Control,* another bottom-feeding effort, where his character was a burnt-out air-traffic controller. Neither was released theatrically in North America. In the U.S., they went directly to video.

14

WORKING STAR

"There were a few years during that time when I literally went from one location to another. I was afraid that if I stopped I would never get another job!"

–Kiefer Sutherland

Actors like Jean Claude Van Damme and Steven Seagal have made a handsome living from direct-to-video films. In some cases Van Damme has earned a fee of up to a third of a film's budget because the producers knew that his name would sell the film around the world. A number of the so-called Brat Pack actors from the early 1980s have surfed these waves as well. Sutherland, however, was not in that league. Although he received top billing in many of his direct-to-video efforts, he took whatever part was available when he was. Yet somehow, he retained an allure, a certain star value. Fellow Canadian Henry Czerny, who co-starred with Sutherland in 1999's *After Alice* (also called *Eye of the Killer* in some markets), puts it this way: "There are a couple of kinds of actors: the stars and the working actors. I am a working actor. That means I take work that is offered to me. I take roles in films, and then it is my job to make the character as convincing as possible. Kiefer, he is a different kind of actor. He is a working star."

After Alice was Sutherland's third direct-to-video film in a row. He was teamed again with Paul Marcus, the director of *Break Up*, and played yet another troubled detective. This time, the cop has sunken into the depths of alcoholism and self-pity after failing, ten years before, to catch a serial killer. Then, to take a break from type, he travelled to the UK to add his voice to those of Stephen Fry, Dawn French, John Hurt, and others for a couple of episodes of the animated series *Watership Down*, based on the best-selling 1972 book.

Back at home, however, the working star had to face the collapse of his second marriage. "Kelly was my best friend," Sutherland says. "I lied to her over and over and again, and it wrecked what we had. The destruction of my second marriage was my doing entirely." The lies that Sutherland was referring to concerned his frequent affairs with other women while away on location. Hardly a master of discretion, he had been confronted by his wife about them numerous times but had tried to deny everything. Finally Winn had enough. The couple separated in mid-1999, although they didn't officially divorce until 2008.

As the century closed, the life of thirty-three-year-old Sutherland was in a shambles. He now had two failed marriages under his belt; he was an absentee father to his only child, Sarah-Jude, something for which he felt very guilty; and although once close to his step-children, he now was no longer part of their lives at all. Professionally, he was scraping bottom. He was still working, but was deriving little satisfaction from it.

His next film was another direct-to home-video outing called *Desert Saints*, a paradigm of the depths to which Sutherland had fallen. The writer-director Richard Greenburg had for years been an assistant director on low-budget films. Deciding he could do no worse than the kinds of films he was working on, Greenburg wrote his own screenplay and raised the money to produce and direct it himself. He tapped his friends, primarily, and credited them as producers. As a result, the film's credits read like a high-school reunion list, which includes the actress Meg Ryan.

The resulting film was forgettable and the script ghastly. Sutherland shared top billing with Melora Walters; the question "Melora who?" says it all. It's not that Melora Walters hasn't paid her dues; she has. Currently a regular on the HBO series *Big Love,* she has played mostly bit parts for over twenty years, beginning with 1989's *Dead Poets Society*. She has appeared in such well-known films as *Beethoven, Ed Wood,* and *Boogie Nights,* but never in a major role. But there she was in *Desert Saints* sharing top billing. For Sutherland, this was far removed from co-starring with Julia Roberts.

In *Desert Saints,* Sutherland plays a world-class hit man named Arthur Banks, who works predominantly for the drug cartels in South America. Banks always recruits lonely, solitary women to assist him in his assignments, then kills them to cover his tracks. On his way to his next job he picks up a woman fleeing an abusive relationship whom he plans to use as his cohort. The FBI is tracking Banks, and he eventually finds out that this woman is not who or what she seems; he genuinely falls for her, and she becomes his Achilles heel and his undoing.

Sutherland does his best with this Tarantino-esque bad guy. He is supposed to be well-spoken and suave in the role, but the dialogue he is given is so poor, and the situations so nonsensical, that everything he tries to do for the character is a wasted effort. And Walters fares no better; she comes off as bland and lacking in depth.

Although Sutherland had now fallen off the A-list with a resounding thud, he was still a part of the Hollywood community. Through his contacts he was invited to join an interesting little indie film where he found a character that he could at last add depth to. *Beat* is the story of Beat Generation writer William S. Burroughs, who is played by Sutherland. Burroughs was a tall, gaunt man in real life, but screenwriter-director Gary Walkow wanted Sutherland to play the writer in his film despite the physical dissimilarities. In Walkow's view, Sutherland had the right kind of intense energy that could be applied to portray the array of passions that raged within Burroughs.

The Beat Generation was a group of American writers living in New York City in the 1950s; they initiated a literary movement by chronicling their bohemian lives of experimenting with drugs, sexual openness, and exploration of Eastern spirituality. In addition to Burroughs's *Naked Lunch,* the most well-known of their works are Jack Kerouac's novel *On the Road,* and Allen Ginsburg's extended poem, *Howl.* Although their output was not great, the Beat writers produced works that shook the literary establishment and laid much of the ground for the social unrest of the U.S. in the 1960s.

Burroughs had a turbulent life. A bisexual, he lived in post-World War II New York City where he got to know Kerouac and Ginsberg. Although intelligent and well-educated, he became a morphine addict and supported himself by dealing heroin. In New York, his second, common-law, wife was Joan Vollmer, herself addicted to amphetamines.

Beat covers a pivotal period in Burroughs's life when he was living in Mexico, having fled the United States to avoid imprisonment for selling marijuana. It was in Mexico that Burroughs experienced the event that was pivotal in making him a writer: his accidental, fatal shooting of Joan Vollmer. The film is appropriately moody and leans heavily on Burroughs's relationships with Vollmer (Courtney Love) and Ginsberg (Ron Livingstone), who has joined them with a mutual friend, writer Lucien Carr (Norman Reedus).

The film was shot in and around Mexico City and had its first showing at the Sundance Film Festival on January 29, 2000. At Sundance, the film generated a lot of buzz, but that didn't translate into the big distribution deal that was hoped for. This was unfortunate, for Sutherland was solid in the film. The worst criticism leveled at him was that he seemed to be doing a Jack Nicholson number on the character. Yet despite the strength of his performance and positive responses at the Los Angeles Independent Film Festival the following April, the film never was able to find a distributor, and the producers had no choice but to send the film straight to video.

Sutherland returned to Canada for his next job—a notable one—in a film called *Woman Wanted*. Though set in New England, the film was shot in Winnipeg, Manitoba. Sutherland was slated to only act in the film, but when creative differences led to the departure of its original director, Sutherland agreed to step in and direct. The credits for the film read "Directed by Kiefer Sutherland, Alan Smithee," the second name being a common pseudonym used by filmmakers who do not want their names to appear on their films.

There was another reason why this film held particular meaning for Kiefer Sutherland; it also featured his mother, Shirley Douglas. When Douglas and Sutherland had acted together before, in a 1997 production of Tennessee Williams's *The Glass Menagerie,* Sutherland had been slightly eclipsed by the talent and experience his mother brought to bear on the stage. Now they were working in film, Sutherland's area of expertise. On top of that, he would be directing his mother; in essence, he would be her creative boss. But

Sutherland found out that some actors don't need much directing, and he would once again defer to his mother's abilities—willingly so, it must be added.

Woman Wanted began as a novel by Joanna McClelland Glass, who adapted her work into the screenplay. The story is a passionate and somewhat bizarre tale about a widower (Michael Moriarty) who lives with his grown son (Kiefer Sutherland) and their relationship with a young live-in housekeeper (Holly Hunter). While Sutherland tried hard to make this film compelling, the final result was a little bland owing to weaknesses in the script. Nevertheless, the atmosphere on-set was good. Canadian actress Jackie Richardson who co-stars, had a wonderful time working on the film: "It was one of those dream jobs for an actor, not necessarily because of the role but because of who you got to go to work with every day—the likes of Kiefer Sutherland and his brilliant mother Shirley Douglas, and Holly Hunter. And it was fun taking direction from Kiefer as well, getting to know him a bit. He was nothing like the guy I expected to meet. He was considerate, polite, and a complete pro."

* * * *

Sutherland began the year 2000 with a miniscule part in one of the most ludicrously misguided filmmaking endeavors of all time; a film that defies logic at nearly every turn. *Picking up the Pieces* concerns a butcher named Tex, played by Woody Allen, who finds his wife Candy (an uncredited Sharon Stone) *in flagrante delicto* with Officer Bobo (Sutherland). Tex proceeds to kill her, chop her up, and strew the pieces across the desert. One of her hands, however, is discovered. Through a set of accidents, holy powers are attributed to it, and the church where it is displayed becomes a pilgrimage destination for the faithful. Enough said.

The film was directed by Mexican-born actor Alfonso Arau, who first gained international attention as a director for his award-winning film *Like Water for Chocolate.* Other cast members include Andy Dick, Elliott Gould, Joseph Gordon-Levitt, Lou Diamond Phillips, David Schwimmer, and Fran Drescher. But neither Arau nor his eclectic cast was able to save what *Variety* reviewer Steven Oxman called a "tawdry misfire of the lowest order." Though it was shot as a feature film, *Picking up the Pieces* was only shown on the pay-cable network Cinemax before heading to video.

Although Sutherland fared no better or worse than anyone else in the film, his appearance in it did nothing but confirm that his movie career was dead in the water. But while everything was fading all around him, he never gave up on himself. As he reflected later, "If a life in show business teaches you anything, it is that you are always one role, one interesting project, or even one phone call away from a complete reversal of fortune—if you continue to believe you are up to it, are in line for it, and if you at least try to always move forward."

* * * *

If at this point in his career Sutherland was stuck in straight-to-video work, at least he was able to choose some enjoyable projects. His first film of 2001 was right up his alley. *Cowboy Up* was about bull-riding, the toughest and most dangerous of rodeo events. The original screenplay, by James Redford, was called *Ring of Fire,* but the title was changed to reflect a catchphrase used by one of the characters in the film. The plot revolves around a rodeo family called the Braxtons. The father, Reid Braxton, is a retired rodeo man, and his two sons are currently working the circuit: Ely is an up-and-coming bull-riding star, and his brother Hank is what is known as a bullfighter, which in North American rodeo parlance means that he is a rodeo clown.

Cowboy Up is a well-intentioned film that comes off like a cross between *Rocky* and *The Champ*, but set in a very different sort of arena. Sutherland plays Hank, and he delivers some of his best acting since *Dark City*. Because Sutherland knew the rodeo world well, he was able to bring a comfortable authenticity to the way his character acts, talks, and views the world; this gave his performance a depth that he hadn't shown for a while. The two female leads in the film are also well struck and well played. Melinda Dillon plays the mother of the two young rodeo cowboys; she is long-suffering and yet both supportive and tough. Molly Ringwald, another Brat Pack alumna, plays Ely's girlfriend with an energy and a passion that is fun to watch.

The set for the Braxton home was the ranch of Rodeo Hall of Fame legend Gary Leffew, and two of Leffew's sons, Judd and Brett, have small roles in the film. Other interesting casting choices include the likes of veteran cowboy star Bo Hopkins playing an old rodeo man and Pete Postlethwaite, the distinguished British stage and screen actor, as Reid Braxton. American Indian activist Russell Means also turns up in the film and later remarked on how Sutherland came across: "I find making movies a very interesting experience," says Means. "*Cowboy Up* I remember because of Kiefer Sutherland and how good he was on a horse and how natural he was around things having to do with animals and the land. He reminds me a bit of Marlon that way." The Marlon to whom Means refers, of course, is Marlon Brando, who, at great personal risk, sheltered Russell Means and fellow American Indian activist Dennis Banks when they were on the run from the FBI during the 1960s.

Sadly, this fine little movie suffered the same fate as most of Sutherland's other recent efforts and languished unreleased for a while before occupying its permanent spot on the lower shelves of the video store racks.

After traveling to Utah to shoot yet one more forgettable effort, *The Right Temptation*, Sutherland headed to Hawaii and Thailand to shoot a compelling film called *To End All Wars*. The film is based on the autobiography of Scottish Captain Ernest Gordon, entitled *Through the Valley of the Kwai*. The book chronicles Gordon's experiences in a Japanese POW camp during World War II, where he was forced to labor under brutal conditions on the construction of the Burma-Thailand Railway.

To *End All Wars* is a beautifully shot film that tells a powerful story. It has similarities to the classic David Lean film *The Bridge on the River Kwai*, which depicted similar events, and in many ways Chubbuck's film serves as a presentation of the facts truth behind the other's fiction. The film's casting is terrific. Scottish actor Ciaran McMenamin plays Gordon, and under different circumstances this film would have made him a star. Fellow Scottish actor Robert Carlyle is also fantastic in the movie. Kiefer Sutherland plays an American POW known as Yankee Reardon, and while his role is similar to the William Holden role in *The Bridge on the River Kwai*, Sutherland creates a character with more poignancy and depth to his character than Holden did.

To End All Wars was first screened to very good reviews at the Telluride Film Festival on September 2, 2001. It was screened again at the Toronto International Film Festival two weeks later to equally strong responses. Unfortunately, it never made it to theatrical release. This had to be disappointing for Sutherland, who delivered a great performance in a film that might have revived his career. Of all the direct-to-video or direct-to-cable films Sutherland made during his time in professional limbo, this one did not deserve that fate.

15

MADE FOR TV

"If you had told me twelve years ago that I would be doing series TV, I wouldn't have thought it even possible—film actors don't do TV. But TV has been my saving grace."

–Kiefer Sutherland

In mid-2000, Sutherland was in Vancouver, British Columbia, filming *Dead Heat,* an action-crime-comedy co-starring Anthony LaPaglia. This was the second time LaPaglia had worked with Sutherland. "I love Kiefer," he says. "Kiefer and I have been on the same kind of journey. We both had our first Hollywood experiences together on *The Mission,* then we made another kind of low-rent movie together with *Dead Heat,* and now we are both known for television work. But what I always think about when I hear his name is how natural acting seems to come to him; he is innately good at it."

When Sutherland returned to California after wrapping *Dead Heat,* television did indeed come beckoning, but it wasn't *24.* In 1999, writer-producer Walon Green, one of the creative minds behind the original *Law and Order* series, had the idea to spin the successful film *L.A. Confidential* into a series for HBO. Green, who wrote such classics as *The Wild Bunch* for Sam Peckinpah and *Sorcerer* for William Friedkin, was struck by the richness of the James Ellroy novel that *L.A. Confidential* was taken from, a tale of cops, crime, corruption, and show business in 1950s Los Angeles. He thought he could create an extended series that would take advantage of all the details and sub-plots of the novel in ways a two-hour feature or limited-run miniseries could not. HBO liked the idea, and Green certainly had the track record to inspire confidence. The director chosen to guide the series was Eric Laneuville, the actor and Emmy-winning television director. Unfortunately, differences over creative control ultimately led HBO to turn down the project. Twentieth Century Fox Television took it up, but they shied away from the big production that Green was advocating. Instead they commissioned a pilot on a far smaller scale and said they would wait and see how it was received.

Despite its limited budget, the pilot turned out very well. It was visually stunning, and Green's screenplay perfectly captured the *noir* flavor of Ellroy's novel. Sutherland was cast in the lead role of Detective Jack Vincennes. Sadly, despite the pilot's strengths, Fox eventually decided not to proceed with the series. But as things evolved, this was fortunate for Sutherland. Had Fox picked up the series and produced a full season's worth of episodes, he would not have been available for the bigger things heading his way.

* * * *

Meanwhile, at Real Time Productions, *24* producers Surnow and Cochran were still trying to cast Jack Bauer and getting nowhere. It was director Stephen Hopkins who eventually suggested

Sutherland. Hopkins knew him personally and was quite familiar with his work. "Kiefer has that rare quality of being able to pull off both the everyman kind of role and the action-star role. And he was not known as a TV actor," says Hopkins. As a matter of fact, the same thing could have been said for Hopkins himself: he had never done a television series before, just music videos and feature films. This turned out to be an advantage; Hopkins did not feel confined to the tried-and-true formulas of television and felt totally free to fashion the show in exactly the way he envisioned it.

When Hopkins called, Sutherland was impressed by the idea of making a weekly show in the manner of a taut feature film. Sutherland recalls, "After Stephen called me, I was intrigued and eager to meet with him, Joel Surnow, and Bob Cochran. I've known Stephen a long time, and I have complete faith in him. That and the fact that he hadn't done TV before made the whole thing very interesting to me."

Sutherland's expectations were low, however, especially in view of the ultimate fate of the *L.A. Confidential* series. He saw that Hopkins was envisioning something yet even more challenging and imagined there were just two likely outcomes: either the concept would not work at all, and the show would fall flat; or it would be fantastic, but too sophisticated for American network television. Either way no one would ever see it. Nevertheless he was determined to give it a try.

Concerns about Sutherland's notoriety as a partier and the lack of distinction of most of his recent work were soon brushed aside. Fox executives were evidently satisfied by the reports on Sutherland's work on the *L.A. Confidential* pilot: he was nothing short of a consummate pro and was a joy to work with.

While the casting of the main characters was left up to Surnow, Cochran, and Hopkins, the then-president of Fox Broadcasting, Gail Berman, had to sign off on their decisions. Berman, who had just assumed the presidency in 2000, was a bit nervous about *24* and had offered an initial contract for the pilot and thirteen episodes only. Berman and her executive team wanted to see how audiences would react to the show before committing to the longer, unorthodox format of a twenty-four-episode series.

Surnow and Cochran had filmed *La Femme Nikita* in Toronto, and at first they assumed at first that *24* would be shot there as well. But the variability of Canadian weather was a problem—for *24*, visual continuity was not just desirable, it was crucial. With each episode happening over the course of a single hour, and with the tight schedules that shooting series television requires, they needed a stable and relatively unchangeable weather pattern. Southern California became the obvious and necessary choice. It was there, mostly at the Real Time Productions studio in the San Fernando Vallley, that the pilot was filmed in March 2001.

* * * *

While waiting for the verdict on the pilot for *24*, Sutherland headed to the other side of the world to make a film that he considers one of his favorites. In May of 2001, he began eight weeks of filming *Paradise Found* in Australia and the Czech Republic. The film recounts the story of the legendary impressionist painter Paul Gauguin, a successful stockbroker in Paris who had everything but what he wanted most: to be an artist. Gauguin eventually left his family and his life in finance to pursue his dream. He traveled to the West Indies and later, famously, to Tahiti, where the natives called him *Oviri*, the savage. The color, light, and space of the Pacific island inspired him to create the works that would re-invent modern art.

There have been only a handful of cinematic depictions of Paul Gauguin, the most famous being by Anthony Quinn, who won an Oscar for his portrayal opposite Kirk Douglas's Vincent van Gogh in 1956's *Lust for Life*. David Carradine also played Gauguin in a rarely-seen but fantastic two-part TV movie called *Gauguin: The Savage*. Then there was a strange little Swedish film that appeared in 1986 from writer-director Henning Carlsen. *Oviri: The Wolf at the Door*, and which featured none other than Donald Sutherland in the role of Paul Gauguin. Kiefer Sutherland says he watched his father's interpretation. "He was fucking amazing. I not only watched my father's version of Gauguin, I studied it. But that film was a depiction of a different time in Gauguin's life . . . when he was friends with August Strindberg."

Sutherland committed himself fully to researching his role. "I did a lot of reading. I read David Sweetman's *Paul Gauguin: A Complete Life* . . . and I spent a while talking to other painters," says Sutherland. His task was to discern what interested him about the artist at the deepest level. "What I needed to know about Gauguin and his influence were things that I'm not well versed in myself, things like how painters view each other, what paintings mean, how to look at them."

There was clearly something about Gauguin that resonated with Sutherland, and indeed there are several striking similarities between the two men. Both are driven artists for whom everything and everyone else is secondary in their lives, both seem unable to resist women, and both abuse themselves with drink—in Gauguin's case, with the notorious absinthe.

Paradise Found was written and directed by Australian filmmaker Mario Andreacchio, and his film is lush and appealing, with Australia standing in for Tahiti and Prague doubling for Paris in the late 1800s. The highlight is Sutherland's passionate and nuanced performance; he is the best Paul Gauguin since Anthony Quinn. Sutherland's portrayal focuses on Gauguin's single-minded determination to create: "He was a great artist with a passion and belief in what he was doing. He gave up everything to follow his passion. I have so much respect for that because I don't have that kind of courage."

"The one thing I understood about Paul Gauguin was that he was consciously trying to create his own legacy," says Sutherland. "He certainly knew that after death it would matter. That was a very big deal to him . . . I think you have to be a son of a bitch in order to dedicate your life to what you're doing, even if you are told how awful you are and know full well that it won't be understood until after you are dead. There is incredible arrogance in that."

It is perhaps that last observation that describes the main difference between the men, however. If there is one thing Sutherland is not, it is arrogant. Yet it is plain from watching Sutherland's performance that he is rendering homage not just to a great artist, but to the consuming passion of creating great art, an emotion he knows all too well.

Once completed, *Paradise Found* languished until March 3, 2003, when it premiered on the big screen at the Adelaide International Film Festival. It was well received, but after a run in Australian cinemas it vanished. It was not seen anywhere in North America until 2007, four years later, when it came out on DVD. And sadly, *Paradise Found*, though a triumph, remains one of the hardest-to-find films of Sutherland's entire career.

Filming of *Paradise Found* had ended in June 2001, and there was good news to greet Sutherland when he returned to the U.S. The pilot for *24* had been well-received by audiences and critics alike, and the producers had received a green light for the first thirteen episodes. Production began in July, and cast and crew worked through the summer to get ready for the show's debut.

Then came September 11, 2001. The events on that day would give the show a dimension no one had anticipated, making it a product of its time in a way no other television program had ever been before. The show had been filming for just over a month, and September 11 began as usual, at 7:00 a.m., with interior scenes being shot on the CTU Los Angeles set. Time stopped, however, at 9:02 a.m. when the first plane hit the World Trade Center in New York City. All of a sudden the cast and crew of *24*, a show about fighting terrorism on domestic soil, found themselves standing around a television screen watching an unprecedented act of real terrorism unfold on the East Coast. Many present had lived or worked or had families in New York, and the show wrapped that day at 10:00 a.m. so everyone could go home.

The Fox legal department promptly reviewed the shows that had already been shot to see if they contained anything that might be unpalatable to the public in the wake of the attacks. In the end, with the exception of a plane blowing up in the first episode, nothing needed to be altered. When *24* debuted on November 6, 2001, the public was more than ready to embrace a show that dealt with terrorism directly.

September 11 confronted the cast and crew of *24* with a reality of terrorism far beyond what its writers had concocted. They were inspired as well. Sutherland in particular took note of the human qualities that the events brought forth: "One thing that moved me to tears was a news clip of three firemen carrying equipment up the stairs of the World Trade Center. They had a look of determination on their faces that was one of the most honorable things I'd ever seen. That unquestioning dedication to duty is something I would love to instill in this character."

But the events were sobering: "I couldn't figure out how to justify how insignificant I felt about making movies or television in the wake of that kind of tragedy, especially compared to the firefighters and police officers and schoolteachers and the people that actually make our society move. About three weeks after the terrorist attacks, somebody came up to me and said, 'Oh man, I can't wait to see *24*.' I almost looked at him and said, 'How could you talk about something so stupid at such a time?' Then I realized—and this took me the rest of the day to figure out—how could you not? You start to look forward to things that will take your mind off of it. So you start again to find your place."

24 found its place. The show was originally scheduled to air on October 30, but because of the disruptions caused by the terrorist attacks on September 11, it had to be delayed a week, to November 6. The premiere episode's reception by the American audience was enthusiastic and showed that, in the wake of the attacks, people were in agreement with the basic premise of the show. The only way to deal with this kind of barbarism was to do it the Jack Bauer way—to take care of business by whatever means necessary.

Just a month later, in late November 2001, and after only three episodes had been shown, Fox President Gail Berman gave the green light for the remaining eleven episodes of Season One. Without necessarily taking anything for granted, the creators of the show now felt that their vision had been vindicated.

All those connected with *24*, especially Surnow, Cochrane, Hopkins, and Sutherland, praised Berman for her guts and vision in backing back the show. "Initially Fox executives Nevins and Berman were so into the show that I was suspicious," says Surnow. "I knew that ultimately this would have to go through some scrutiny from the Fox board. But Gail Berman backed us to the hilt, and we were able to do the show our way."

* * * *

To keep audiences connected to the various simultaneous plot lines, the producers and director Hopkins developed techniques—split-screen visuals and traveling boxes within the frame—to enable the show to maintain the fast-paced tension of the main action while allowing the personal lives of the characters to play out in parallel, all in real time. This gave *24* unusual depth.

The show works as well as it does because it is extremely well-written. Critical plot elements, like an imminent threat, a character's duplicity, or a deliberate red herring, have to be unveiled quickly but logically to fit into the twenty-four-hour day. And they have to be solidly grounded in reality. Many films and television shows, from the Bond movies to *Lost,* often stretch reality for the sake of entertainment. *24* does not have that luxury; it has to have a basis in reality at every moment or the credibility of the whole premise falls apart.

The pilot had set the mold for the show's whole run, including the three-act format: It began with CTU agent Jack Bauer introducing himself in a voice-over-narration and telling the audience that what they were about to witness took place over a one-hour period: from midnight to 1:00 a.m. on the morning of the California presidential primary. When the first season began in earnest, the story unfolded on several levels: a plot to assassinate a presidential candidate; the related kidnapping of Bauer's daughter, Kim; and the discovery of a mole within the CTU team.

The assembly of the initial cast of *24* seemed to be blessed—every casting decision in that first season ended up being dead-on perfect; each match seemed to allow the actor to display his or her best. (An odd coincidence in the casting is that the pivotal characters in that first year—Jack Bauer, his wife Teri, and daughter Kim—are all played by Canadian actors.)

Elisha Cuthbert, who plays Kim Bauer, left her Montreal home at the age of seventeen to give Hollywood a try. Born in Calgary, Alberta, Cuthbert was raised in the town of Longueuil, Quebec, just east of Montreal. She arrived in Los Angeles in 2001 with a self-imposed deadline of six weeks to land some kind of acting job. A month of auditions and readings went by with no luck. Then, in week five, she auditioned for the production team of *24* and was offered the part of Jack Bauer's daughter.

Cuthbert and Sutherland got along famously from day one, largely because of their shared passion for hockey. "Elisha and I can always get into a good argument about hockey," he says. "And the amazing thing is, she's an expert on the game, so it is hard to win any of those arguments." Cuthbert's passion for hockey ranges from her contribution of a blog on the NHL.com site called Hollywood Hockey Thoughts to her season tickets to the Los Angeles Kings to her well-publicized romances with New York Ranger bad boy Sean Avery and Calgary Flames defenseman Dion Phaneuf.

The actress cast as Teri Bauer, Leslie Hope, was born in Halifax, Nova Scotia, and made her debut as an actress in 1981 almost by accident. She was attending St. Michaels University School in

Victoria, British Columbia, when the school allowed Canadian director Paul Almond to shoot his film *Ups & Downs* there. He agreed to use some of the students in his film, and Leslie Hope won a role.

The character of Teri Bauer was a demanding one to play; she goes through the cyclone of having her daughter kidnapped, then being kidnapped herself and raped and beaten to the point of amnesia. The producers were looking for an actress capable of displaying a wide range of emotions while depicting deep physical and mental strength. Leslie Hope came through with the combination of emotion and toughness they needed.

One of the non-Canadian standouts from the first season is Dennis Haysbert, who was cast as presidential hopeful Senator David Palmer. Haysbert is a towering presence as an actor, not just because he measures in at 6’4” but also because he has one of the richest baritone voices since James Earl Jones. He has been a steadily working actor since his first appearance on the television show *Lou Grant* in 1978. Since then he has appeared on series television, has been a regular on the soap opera *The Young and the Restless,* and has performed in high-profile feature films such as *Heat,* opposite Robert DeNiro and Al Pacino, and the Iraq-war film *Jarhead,* with Jamie Foxx. He has also been a favorite of indie film directors. Writer-director Todd Haynes cast Haysbert in his poignant 2002 film about passion and race relations in the 1950s, *Far from Heaven*. Scheduling conflicts arose when Haysbert found himself committed to shooting both *Far from Heaven* in New Jersey and the second season of *24* in California. Luckily, the producers of both thought him valuable enough that they were willing to schedule his work days so he could shuttle back and forth to act in each.

"The thing I loved about *24* from the start," said Haysbert in 2002, "was that everything Surnow, Cochran, and Hopkins were trying to do was in direct contravention with what was commonplace in series television. I thought that what we were doing was bold, but I did wonder if the audience out there would embrace all the things about the show that they weren't used to. I hoped they would, and I was tending towards giving the public more credit than most did. So I was delighted when the show took off, but not shocked, because I believe the show is that good."

Breaking conventions on television may have had reverberations in real life. Haysbert's portrayal of Palmer, who in Season Two becomes the first black president of the U.S., is considered by many to have eased the way for current U.S. President Barack Obama to do it for real six years later.

* * * *

As Season One progressed, Hopkins, as the director, essentially designed the look of the show and set the tone for the writing. His template would hold long after he was no longer a part of the show. "The idea of creating the boxes, the split-screen effect, in order to keep the clarity and the urgency of the story, that was all Stephen Hopkins," says Sutherland. "I thought that was ingenious. That stuff was not in the script, and now it is used in music videos and commercials and even on the news."

The real-time facet of the show, which producers feared might come across as a gimmick, was embraced as an effective tension-building device. The show was directed with style, yet the show's visual impact did not get in the way of the story. The performances were astounding across the board. All of this was accomplished in an atmosphere that was more like movie-making than television. "That first [half] season of TV for me was quite an eye-opener," Sutherland remembers. "It was like shooting twelve feature films in a row without stopping—twelve particularly demanding feature films!"

Hopkins directed twelve episodes of that first season, with two other directors, Winrich Kolbe and Bryan Spicer, taking the reins for the rest. Cochran and Surnow were closely involved in writing many of the first season's episodes, assisted by Howard Gordon, who took on a more prominent role in future seasons, and Michael Loceff and Chip Johannessen. It was this creative team that established the unique look and feel of the show, which has remained consistent despite subsequent changes in personnel.

What set *24* apart from most other dramatic television series was the way it deliberately kept the audience off-balance with a constantly high level of tension. This was expressed most clearly in the producers' readiness to kill off major characters. The ending to Season One is a case in point; Stephen Hopkins argued against killing off Teri Bauer, but the producers maintained that it was the type of event the series needed to strike a chord. To this day, Hopkins remains unconvinced: "I thought and I still think that killing Teri Bauer was the wrong thing to do. The family dynamic is what made Jack an interesting man. It was through that family dynamic that he was seen to be a flawed but decent man, a loving man at his core. Killing his wife like that would give him every valid reason to become a much different, darker, and changed man." But Joel Surnow was thinking about the audience in a different way: "A happy ending would not have been in keeping with the never-know-what-is-going-to-happen-next atmosphere that we had established with the show."

The producers went so far as to shoot an alternative in which Teri survives. But it didn't feel right. "It was almost like we were making a kind of subliminal decision to sabotage that alternative happy ending," says Surnow. "Everything from the shooting to the blocking, the writing, and the acting just felt clunky and awkward. It is a good thing we didn't use it because it would have been a bad way all around to end a great first season."

Sutherland was very disappointed. "That was the toughest part about Season One," he says. "I lost my right hand. Leslie Hope is one of the most incredible actors in the world. She's a friend. She had the other story line, and I never had to worry about that. Literally, I got to the point where I could start reading my own stuff and not even worry about what her stuff was, because I knew we were safe. I lost someone I loved working with very much."

* * * *

In the fall of 2001, after the first thirteen episodes were shot, everyone involved believed they had done something unique and were anxiously looking forward to the premiere. But all actors know that the world of television and film is fickle; one never knows what an audience will respond to at any given time. Sutherland was hopeful about *24*, but was not holding his breath. "I thought it was great, and I hoped it would turn into something," he says. "But until it did, I had to keep on working and looking for interesting projects to do."

Just in case, Sutherland had lined up two projects to follow the taping of the first half of *24*. But as soon as the show aired, it became an instant hit both with audiences and with critics. Its ratings were spectacular, and the awards followed. In just its first season, the show received Golden Globe and Emmy nominations for technical achievements, and for acting and directing. Sutherland won a Golden Globe for best actor in a dramatic television series—not bad for his first foray into series television. The show did not win any Emmys that year, but that would certainly change in the seasons to come.

Had Sutherland broken his run of bad luck? Or was this just a temporary respite due to a few lucky choices? *Time* magazine called *24* "the television event of the decade," while the *New York Times* praised Sutherland's performance, saying, "[He] is so good in this role that you forget he is actually acting." Sutherland didn't intend to sit still long enough to consider this. When he won the Golden Globe, he says, "my mind went totally blank and my body went numb. It was a very surreal moment . . . It was a great night. I admit I felt really cocky for about twenty-four hours, then I went back to work."

16

LUCKY MAN

"I would have to say that this has been the luckiest year of my entire life."

–Kiefer Sutherland

In the time of excited anticipation after shooting the pilot and first episodes of *24* in 2001 and what was to be the explosion of the *24* phenomenon in 2002, Kiefer Sutherland's career and personal life coasted along more or less as they had been. He was still living life from one film location to another, partying hard, and getting into the odd scrape at hotel bars. Though committed to *24*, Sutherland was not one to sit still or to bank too heavily on any one thing. So, in early 2002, after the final eleven episodes of Season One were completed, he took on a couple of other projects to keep things moving. Because of *24*'s severely demanding schedule, they were the last feature films he did for a long time.

The first of these came out of a pleading phone call from Joel Schumacher, the director he had had the most success with over the years. Sutherland never turned Schumacher down if he could help it, and this time was no exception. The film in question was *Phone Booth*, which had been in gestation for some forty years. It was an unusual project in every way. The premise concerns an egotistical, mendacious PR man who is trapped in a Manhattan phone booth by a deranged sniper who seems to know everything about him. The sniper forces the PR man, played by Colin Farrell, to come clean with everyone he has deceived. He must do this in front of the media, and if he hangs up the phone or tries to leave the phone booth he will be shot. The caller (Kiefer Sutherland) demonstrates his sincerity by firing a few rounds at people in the vicinity.

Larry Cohen wrote the screenplay for *Phone Booth* in the mid-1960s and pitched it to Alfred Hitchcock. The great director declined to take on the project at the time because of a flaw in the plot: they were unable to develop a credible pretext for keeping the PR man pinned down in the phone booth. Years later, in the late 1990s, Cohen came up with the idea that a high-tech sniper rifle was a believable means to keep a victim inside a phone booth.

When the screenplay was picked up by 20th Century Fox, action director Michael Bay showed some interest, but he wanted to expand the action outside of the phone booth. This would have completely altered the concept, and Fox wanted to keep to the original premise of the arrogant man trapped in the phone booth. The film was brought to director Joel Schumacher, who loved the idea. Schumacher saw *Phone Booth* as an experimental bit of movie making, much like his film *Tigerland* a couple of years earlier. "Here was a big studio film that I was planning to shoot in just twelve working days," says Schumacher. "It was a thriller in which you never really saw the bad guy, and you would be watching the story unfold in real time."

Mel Gibson was interested in working on the film and did some development with Schumacher on the script; a number of Gibson's ideas made it into the final film. Will Smith and Jim Carrey were also briefly involved. When Carrey dropped out, Schumacher asked Colin Farrell, his *Tigerland* discovery, to do it.

Farrell portrays the unlikeable PR man well; he is a better actor than people generally give him credit for. But it is the chilling performance by Sutherland, achieved almost entirely with his voice alone, that makes this film so taut and exciting. The actor Ron Eldard originally appeared as the caller, but while Eldard is a capable actor, he did not capture the malevolence that Schumacher wanted. "I remember thinking that I needed a voice like Kiefer's," Schumacher says. "Then I thought, why not? I gave Kiefer a call. He really made me crazy; he wouldn't let me tell him what it was about."

Sutherland recalls the conversation: "It was a funny situation. I'd known about the film for a long time, but I didn't know that it had actually been made. Then Joel called me up to see if I was interested. He started to talk, and I said, 'Yes,' and he said, 'Let me finish my sentence!' "

Schumacher was relieved by Sutherland's approach to the task at hand. It was December 2001, and Sutherland was riding high on the news that the last half of the first season of *24* had been given the go-ahead. "Kiefer came in and basically just asked how fast, what tone, what is he thinking?" says Shumacher. "We sat down and watched the film, and then he did each take damn near perfectly." About the re-filming, Farrell recounts, "I never met Kiefer at all. When I saw the film it was pretty creepy because the voice I [had been] hearing on the telephone [during filming] was not Kiefer's voice; it didn't have his edge and his intelligence. I actually got caught up in the film as a viewer because of Kiefer's voice."

Sutherland received second billing in the film despite appearing on screen for fewer than three minutes. "It was the most amazing thing," he remembers. "I recorded my part in a voice booth even though the movie is not an animated film. It was a unique situation, and I loved it." His image did not appear on the original one sheet—the movie poster—but when the film was released on video, his face was added to the artwork.

Although *Phone Booth* was shot in November and December 2001, it was only released in late 2002. That didn't stop it from making over $15 million on its opening weekend alone, though. It was a bona-fide hit, the first Sutherland had had in a long time. Produced for $10 million, the film went on to make almost $50 million at the domestic box office. It was another successful Schumacher-Sutherland collaboration.

Six months later, in June 2002, Sutherland took advantage of the summer break in the *24* schedule to return briefly to Canada, to the rugged Atlantic province of Newfoundland, to shoot the film *Behind the Red Door.* Alongside co-stars Kyra Sedgwick and Stockard Channing. Sutherland plays narcissistic Roy, a gay Boston fashion designer who is dying of AIDS. His estranged sister Natalie (Sedgwick) is a photographer in New York who has been struggling of late. Roy wants to use his final days to reconnect with her and so he secretly hires her for a well-paid gig in Boston. When she finds out who hired her and why, she stays on and reconciles with her brother during his final days. In the process she is forced to confront lingering family secrets.

Although both Sutherland and Sedgwick deliver fine, measured performances, their characters are not that sympathetic, and their struggles to come to terms with the time they have lost fail to resonate with the viewer. The rugged Newfoundland scenery, standing in for New England, makes the film visually interesting, but in the final analysis all it amounted to was another straight-to-DVD entry in

Sutherland's filmography. In a way it was a cap on the long, thankless period of Sutherland's creative life before *24*, because from now on, he was a star to be reckoned with.

****

In late summer 2002, the highly anticipated second season of *24* went into production with dissent in the creative ranks. Writer-director Stephen Hopkins had left at the end of the first season. He had deeply disagreed with Joel Surnow and Robert Cochran about killing off the character of Teri Bauer and was unhappy with the political nuances of the story for Season Two. Joel Surnow is a hard-core conservative and a close friend of notorious right-wing radio host Rush Limbaugh. The show strongly reflects Surnow's own political views, and while he didn't want to see Hopkins leave the show, he was determined to lead *24* in the direction that he and Cochran had envisioned.

The second season was to be more violent and aggressively political than the first. The plot line concerned a Middle Eastern terrorist group about to detonate a nuclear bomb in Los Angeles. The first act would depict the CTU and the White House trying to prevent the terrorists from setting off the bomb. The second act would expose the real masterminds behind the plot, people from a lot closer to home, just as the U.S. government was planning a retaliatory strike against the Middle Eastern country supposedly aiding the terrorists. Although the storyline was conceived and written well before the United States invaded Iraq, the similarities are striking. The critical difference was that in the fictional version the CTU was trying to prevent the U.S. from taking action that it knew was a mistake.

Surnow swears that the similarity of the show's storyline with real-life events was strictly coincidental. "We got a little weirdly synchronized during Season Two when the United States was ramping up for war" he says. "That was just an accidental thing, a matter of timing." Season Two's executive producer, Evan Katz, echoes that sentiment: "The second season had a lot to do with fomenting war in the Middle East under false pretenses. We had no idea that the U.S. was going to be taking up a war with Iraq at that time. It was eerie when we saw it really happening as we were in production. We knew that people would think we were making a comment on what was really happening, but we thought this stuff up long before it really occurred."

Stephen Hopkins's departure as the creative driving force on the set made way for the addition of Jon Cassar. Yet another Canadian, Cassar was born in Malta but was raised in Ontario, Canada, where he began his career as a cameraman and Steadicam operator. He made his directorial debut on a film called *The Final Goal* in 1994, but it was his directorial work on the TV series *La Femme Nikita* from 1997 through 2001 that brought him into contact with Joel Surnow and Robert Cochran.

As Cassar became a major influence in the creative direction of *24,* he also became close friends with Sutherland, who was now himself a producer of the show. "As much as I hated to see Stephen leave the show, we were most fortunate to have a guy like Jon come on board," says Sutherland. "Jon didn't just keep it going, he upped the ante with each show and each season. The thing about Jon that makes him a big part of the show's success is that he always has the audience, the fans, in the forefront of his thought process."

Two new main female characters were added to the show for Season Two. Reiko Aylesworth joined the cast as junior CTU agent

Michelle Dessler, the romantic interest of the CTU acting director, Tony Almeida. She had interviewed for other roles on the show: originally for the role of Nina Myers, which was given to Sarah Clarke, and then for the other new role, Kate Warner, which was assigned to Sarah Wynter. But Cassar and fellow producer Sutherland saw an on-screen chemistry between Reiko and Carlos Bernard (Almeida), and cast her in a role she hadn't even auditioned for. Later, in 2005, Sutherland and Aylesworth dated for a short period.

At this point, the people at Fox Broadcasting knew they had a popular hit on their hands. The show was well received critically and had gained a mass audience, but the network was nevertheless concerned that the real-time, edge-of-your-seat gimmick could not be sustained. They felt the show would be better served with stand-alone episodes. One of the *24*'s producers, Howard Gordon, remembers, "They actually wanted us to try scripting a stand-alone-type scenario for each episode, and we felt obligated to attempt it." Sutherland objected strongly to the network's request. "That would have killed the show. We did work on the scripts. But we didn't apply all that much ingenuity or effort to it, so that when we turned in the scripts to the network, they would clearly see that *24* would not work in the way they were suggesting." Sutherland was very concerned about the audience. "We had built a solid fan base very quickly, and those fans made the show a success; had we turned on them, it would have ended the show for sure." Ultimately, Season Two proceeded with its by-now trademark hour-by-hour format.

Director Jon Cassar was the regular director on the show, although he did not direct everything himself; cinematographer Rodney Charters was bumped up to director for a few episodes mid-season, and other directors to take the helm were James Whitmore Jr., son of the late actor James Whitmore, and Ian Toynton, whose work on Season Two was nominated for an Emmy.

When the first episode of Season Two aired in October 2002, it was shown without commercial interruptions; the Ford Motor Company bought all the commercial time and ran their ads before and after the episode. This was the beginning of a long relationship between *24* and Ford, which employed Sutherland as a spokesperson as well.

The reaction to the new season was strong. The show was responding to the climate of the times and the audience rewarded *24* with its devotion. And yet, Sutherland comments, "real-life events and events as they unfolded on the show drew dramatically apart in the second season. Our show was all about stopping a war, whereas real-life events were about rushing into a war." Co-creator and executive producer Joel Surnow echoes the sentiment: "I think the war in Iraq really hurt the show. It looked like we were commenting on the way things really were, but we were creating entertainment. We are as topical as we can be, but we are still entertainment at the end of the day. A lot of what we thought up just made sense to the story and had nothing to do with what was going on in the geo-political world outside."

Critics of Season Two singled out the new violence as a disturbing development. The torture of Jack Bauer was extreme. In that scene, Sutherland was hung up naked, gagged, and was electrocuted; everyone involved in shooting the scene found it very disturbing, especially Sutherland, who called it a "very rough day." In addition to the graphic display of torture, there was a great deal more gunplay in Season Two. The realism is underscored by the fact that every gun seen on screen is a real, unloaded weapon. In Sutherland's case, it is a 9mm Heckler & Koch compact pistol. The sole exception is the stuntmen, who use rubber replicas so as not to hurt themselves or damage the expensive weapons during falls.

The depiction of violence in Season Two reaches its climax in a scene toward the end of the season. Kim Bauer is being menaced by a man she works for. She trains a gun on him after knocking him out and is on the phone with her father, who urges her to shoot the man. Kim shoots the man in the chest, whereupon Bauer urges her to shoot him again. The graphic quality of a father telling his teenage daughter to fire a gun at an unconscious man, twice, in order to kill him, raised some critical eyebrows.

* * * *

Part of what keeps *24* viewers on the edge of their seats is that they never know what is coming next. Part of this is deliberate; precipitous acts of violence and the sudden killing-off of established characters are used to maintain the tension and excitement. But some of this unpredictability is a consequence of the way the show is produced. As Sutherland explains, "We shoot two episodes back to back. It takes about fifteen days to shoot them, with shooting days of at least twelve hours. Often the next few episodes haven't even been written yet, so we always have to be in the moment." Joel Surnow adds, "By the time we actually shoot an episode we have already done between ten and fifteen drafts. We end up writing some of the best scenes after parts of the script are shot. When it's being edited we see where there are gaps or where things need to be stitched together, so we write these great scenes to tighten the show up."

For an actor as skilled as Sutherland, this is what helps him make his characterization of Jack Bauer so utterly believable. "I know generally where the arc of the story is going," he says, "but the scripts are constantly being revised. A lot of them, especially the final episode, come to me without an ending. It forces me to play the scene without knowing where things are going. I have to just play the moment, play the situation. I really believe that having the ability to act instinctually like that is what makes the difference between something that is really good and something that isn't."

The quality of the acting on *24* is helped by the chemistry among the actors. One particularly poignant scene is the heartbreaking goodbye conversation that Jack and his daughter Kim have together; he is on a plane, she, in a car. When episode director Ian Toynton was shooting Jack Bauer's part of the conversation, Elisha Cuthbert was in fact lying in the back of the plane set speaking her lines to him. Later, when they shot Kim's scenes in the car, where she is carrying on her side of the conversation, Sutherland was crouched in the back of the car speaking his lines to her.

To maintain secrecy, scripts for *24* are printed on red paper so they cannot be photocopied—some actors find them hard to read and study from. And despite the ongoing script changes, the show is carefully prepared. For a fight scene Jack has with a thug in the L.A. Coliseum, a fight lasting fewer than thirty seconds on screen, Sutherland and the stuntman working with him rehearsed the scene and its marital arts components for four days. "These fight scenes are like learning a complicated dance," says Sutherland. "And I am the weak partner in the dance; I have to learn every movement."

During the final, climactic fight scene of Season Two, Sutherland was cut near his left eye. He bled, was treated, and then went back at it with stuntman J. J. Perry. The stuntman had praise for Sutherland: "He's a pretty tough guy. He was leaking like a prizefighter, but he wanted to keep going. Most actors I work with just completely collapse when they're bumped even a bit, but Kiefer took it. He always takes it. Good for him."

That wasn't the only injury to befall Sutherland in the second season. On one occasion, after a long day of shooting, Kiefer was having a few drinks in his trailer. When it came time to leave, he misjudged the steps and badly injured his ankle. An explanation for why Jack Bauer was limping then had to be written into the show. Sutherland was also fitted with a special boot that successfully disguised the cast he was wearing.

Sutherland the producer and Sutherland the actor were increasingly committed to the success of the show. He was wholly hands-on with regard to the show's look, to how the episodes unfolded, and to the actors' well-being. At the end of Season Two, in the spring of 2003, Sutherland was the last of the actors to finish. He was needed until the very end to do pick-up shots and make sure everything was covered. After the wrap, he hugged his crew members one by one—crew members who approached him with an outstretched hand to shake would have their hand knocked away and be warmly embraced. Sutherland told each that it had been an honor to work with them. He also made sure that all the crew drank on his tab on that last night of shooting. "Everybody has to have at least one," was his invitation. And since there was a bar next door to the San Fernando Valley soundstage, he left work that night telling everyone, "I'll see you next door!" It was well-known among the crew that Sutherland loved to drink Jack Daniels and Coca-Cola. He could put them away like a champ. Although he would get tipsy fast, he could keep on downing drinks until he could barely stand up.

While Sutherland was known for his hard drinking, though, he was gaining a solidly positive reputation for his efforts on *24*. For the second year in a row he was nominated for best actor in a dramatic television series at the Golden Globes. And the show and its crew were again nominated for many Golden Globes and Emmys.

Sutherland's career reclamation was now complete; he was once again a sought-after player. But if he had renewed himself professionally, his drunkenness continued to grow in frequency and intensity. As Sutherland himself frames it, "I work really hard with very long hours on the show. So if at the end of a long, tough day or week I choose to go out with some friends and do some drinking and blow off some steam and sometimes do stupid things, well, I have to live with that. But that is what I do."

17

JACK BAUER

"One of the big draws of the show is here's a guy who is ordinary in many ways, but, due to his profession, he's placed in extraordinary situations that he has to make right with action and with thought. That's what is appealing about Jack—he takes charge."

–Kiefer Sutherland

By the end of its second season, in May 2003, *24* was not just a hit, it was a phenomenon. The success of the show had to do with many things: the genius of its creators, the talent of its writers, and the willingness of everyone involved to take risks, to do things never previously done on television. The timing was good as well; the early plots bore an eerie similarity to actual events that the writers could not have predicted. In the wake of 9/11, the audience, too, was ready for *24* in a way they might not have been otherwise.

The actors, of course, were crucial. They interpreted their roles to give credibility to characters who could easily have become caricatures in less capable hands. Over time, the cast of *24* has changed completely; only one actor aside from Sutherland has been with the show during its entire run. It follows that, if the success of *24* were to be attributed to one person, it would be the person producer Howard Gordon singled out as the "heart and soul" of the show at the 2006 Emmy Awards: Kiefer Sutherland.

Sutherland became Jack Bauer—Sutherland *is* Jack Bauer—in a way no one else could be. He has infused the character with a personality, mannerisms, and a voice that are impossible to imagine anyone duplicating. But it goes beyond that—Sutherland has created a new version of the American icon that started with the cowboy. It is his life itself, his personal journey, that has enabled him to give it form. It is likely that the Jack Bauer we know would have been inaccessible to anyone who hadn't shared Sutherland's background. Bauer and *24* might have ended up a successful TV program, but not likely an iconic one. That is Sutherland's unique contribution.

Many shows, once they have achieved success, become formulaic. The characters ease into a comfortable predictability that Hollywood executives feel their audiences want. To their credit, the producers of *24* have never thought that way, although they occasionally succumbed to gimmickry in order to maintain each season's intensity. What held together the show's integrity was Sutherland's performance of Jack Bauer.

Unlike most shows or films, *24* actors must seem credibly real at all times in order for the concept to work. In many other shows, this not as important as long as the entertainment value is there. The *24* format is a nearly impossible one: Bauer could not walk away from each episode and each season untouched, with every hair in place, to begin again next year. What kept audiences rapt was Bauer's ability to be a simple human being, doing things no person should be asked to do. If his human frailty is undermined, the show collapses.

This moral tension keeps the Bauer character from reverting into a Hollywood stereotype, and it is Sutherland's skill that gives this tension depth.

In a way, the production schedule itself helped reinforce the show's intensity by giving Sutherland the consistent working environment he likes and needs. Sutherland himself describes it thus: "We work ten months a year, opposed to the standard eight. We shoot for twelve to fourteen hours per day, five days per week, then do prep work on the weekends. Toward the end of the season we get into working hard nights, which means we work from 5 p.m. until 5 a.m." A half-hour comedy, by contrast, shoots four days a week, many of which are half days.

* * * *

The moral quandaries in the show do not come from the villains, who are as irredeemably bad as the writers can convincingly make them. The threats Jack Bauer has faced have come from Islamist terrorists, Mexican drug dealers, Russian militants, and from traitors within the U.S. There is never any sense that Bauer is on the wrong side. Rather, his dilemma is to reconcile his extreme behavior—the solutions he is forced to come up with—with what he knows to be morally correct. The "right thing to do" becomes disputable and ambiguous and it tears him apart.

It is the humanity of Jack Bauer at the heart of *24*, and from the first episode, his ability to retain his humanity in the face of adversity that is challenged. Season One sees Bauer's family threatened from the outset. His wife is kidnapped, then his daughter, then both. The race to save a political figure, his duty as an officer in the employ of the U.S. government, plays out in parallel and conflicts with his duty to protect his family. His personal and professional duties pull at him, and in the end, he succeeds at one, only to partially fail at the other. His daughter lives; his wife,however, is killed.

In the second season, he loses his daughter, not to death, but to resentment. They become estranged. Bauer, in turn, holds his employers to blame for his family tragedy. Yet his sense of duty pulls him yet again to perform his job.

Even at this stage it is evident that the themes of family loss would resonate with Sutherland. With two divorces and the accompanying awareness he was responsible for them, compounded with the guilt of living apart from a daughter he loved, there is little doubt that Sutherland brought to Bauer emotions derived from personal experience.

Season Three had difficulties in maintaining the momentum from the first two seasons. Bauer exacts revenge, killing the treacherous agent who robbed him of his beloved wife. He re-connects with his daughter, though in the course of that he mutilates his future son-in-law, cutting off his hand. Again, in the service of the nation, Bauer saves millions of lives but cuts another scar into his family.

Bauer is fighting addiction as well in Season Three. He became a heroin addict as part of an undercover operation and is in the middle of trying to quit cold turkey. Sutherland received critical praise for his portrayal of the agony of kicking heroin. "I thought it was a great idea, the addiction and the withdrawal," he says. "What concerned me about that from an acting standpoint was how to articulate that experience properly in a twenty-four-hour period."

To ensure accuracy, Sutherland researched heroin addiction extensively. He spoke to doctors about the realities of addiction. He also had sources of information closer to home: "Unfortunately I have a close friend who had a serious problem with this kind of thing. He has been free of it for ten years now, but I did talk to him a lot about what this looks and feels like." Although it is standard for actors to undertake this sort of background research, it is characteristic of Sutherland's approach to acting that he found someone he knew who had suffered and created a personal connection to the experience he was trying to portray and no doubt his own difficulties with alcohol contributed to his understanding.

In what has become a pattern, because one of the season's scenes shot in a prison was so violent and disturbing, Sutherland recorded a public-service announcement sponsored by Americans for Gun Safety, which was aired at the end of the episode.

The season resorted to some polished, yet unreal plot turnings that were convenient for the storyline, but not, in the end, very credible. Nevertheless, the creative team managed to re-establish the show's aura of reality, and hence its credibility, by the final episode. As Sutherland, now elevated to co-producer, put it, "Our concern at this point, as much as broadening the show, was maintaining the quality and the innovative things that the writers had established as the norm. We weren't so much concerned with always getting better and better; we were concerned with not backsliding, not getting worse."

The powerful final scene of Season Three embodies not just Bauer, but Sutherland, and reinforces the archetype hero that he has created. At first, the producers had no idea what they were going to do. "Jon [director Jon Cassar] and I messed around with that a bit," says Sutherland. "When we got to this point at the end of the season we really didn't have a clue where we were going with Bauer."

Alone in his car, Bauer breaks down under the weight of all the emotions of the day and of the past years. But the phone rings, and he composes himself and answers. It is another call to duty. He pulls himself together, and he obeys. This rivetting ending is a testament to the relationship between Sutherland and Cassar. "I trust Jon implicitly," says Sutherland. "When I just allowed myself to completely break down on camera and let everything just pour out—when I get in that place I am kind of lost in it. So when it was done and I was able to pull myself together, I asked Jon how it went. He simply said, 'You got it, we're done.' "

This was a pivotal moment for *24*, confirming its focus on the character of Jack Bauer and on the progression of his internal torment and conflicts. Sutherland said afterward, "I think the key to the popularity and interest in this character is that he is still growing and evolving in many ways." He adds, "Every season Jack is allowed to carry with him what he has suffered the year before. The repercussions of his choices allow me as an actor to have incredibly personal emotional responses."

* * * *

Season Four delves more deeply into moral ambiguity. It also casts Bauer into emotional isolation. As producer Robert Cochran explained, "With [Jack Bauer's daughter] Kim written out of the show, Bauer has no real emotional connection to anyone. That would make him too much of a free floater. We needed to have him emotionally attached, so he has something to care about other than his job. So, we thought of the idea of having him in love with a woman. Because the events of the last season were so traumatic, he heads off and tries to change his life completely."

Sutherland agreed. "It is impossible for an audience to continually follow a character that is always starting from a place of such deep despair," he says. "You have to want him to get through the day for some reason, and love is the greatest reason of all. If there is a love interest, the audience will buy that he has something to fight for, something worth living for." This was done to keep Bauer's humanity up front while the scripts had him behaving in increasingly inhuman ways. In true *24* fashion, however, Bauer's love interest would prove more a source of pain than solace for him, and the relationship does not last.

The choice of villains in Season Four was, again, Islamist extremists. "I knew we were going to take some heat for that," says Joel Surnow. "But let's face it, we looked around at what was happening in the world and, yes, Islamic extremism is something this country and many other free-world countries are having to deal with constantly."

This decision led Sutherland to record another public service announcement, this time in cooperation with the Council on Islamic Relations. In the announcement, he clarifies that that the show was not condemning all Muslim people. "We were never being overtly racist," says Sutherland. "Our story line had to do with radicalism, and, really, radical fundamentalist terrorists are generally coming out of the Middle East. We aren't making this stuff up. We didn't once imply that we felt all people of Middle Eastern origin or all Muslim people were to be automatically suspected."

Season Five is generally considered to be the best one thus far. Though the previous season had been satisfactory, producers Surnow, Cochran, Gordon, and Sutherland were determined to bring a fresh spin to the program. They knew their fan base was solid and could weather some change. Joel Surnow remembers, "We had been working on a storyline for weeks, then someone just spoke up one day and said, 'What if ex-President Palmer was assassinated suddenly because he had some knowledge of a potential attack on the way?' So we scrapped everything we had and went with that idea. We started shooting the show with only enough content for four episodes; that was it. After episode four, we were winging it." Robert Cochran adds, "We had no idea where we were going with this season, so it is amazing it all came together and that we would win all those awards and score the highest ratings the show had ever had. We literally had nothing [at the beginning of the season]."

Briefly, Bauer, who is being hunted by the Chinese, emerges from hiding for a purely personal reason: to track down the terrorists who have killed his friend, former president Palmer, who was played by Dennis Haysbert. "At the beginning we tried to set it up so that even if Jack was not content, he at least was temporarily satisfied with his life in hiding," says Surnow. "An ongoing theme of the show is that Jack Bauer has a fate that he cannot escape, no matter what happens. He even tried to kill himself to escape that, and it still didn't work."

It turns out that the current American president is behind the assassination of his predecessor. Depicting the downfall of the president of the United States is something that all four producers remain steadfast about, Sutherland especially. "I have always been really proud of our writers for tackling controversial material head on and not backing down from it," he says. "The idea that we would have to placate the audience on any level because they can't 'get' something is absolutely wrong. Our audience is incredibly smart."

Once it was established that not only ex-president Palmer would get killed but also several other main characters, some of whom had been with the show since the beginning, even the normally risk-friendly Howard Gordon was concerned: "I was wondering if we were committing a kind of artistic suicide here. It was starting to feel like the end of *The Godfather* where everyone gets killed off all at once right at the end!"

Inevitably, Sutherland had to set the standard, and he did. To the cast and crew of *24*, he had become the iron backbone the show rested on. His co-stars attest to his professionalism. According to Peter Weller, of *Robocop* fame, "The intensity of Kiefer Sutherland is what I remember from that gig. There's a scene that has Jack Bauer holding my character and his wife at gunpoint. I'm telling Jack that he can shoot me if he wants, but I won't tell him anything. Without a beat he turns the gun and fires a bullet into my wife's leg. It was so intense, and Kiefer never broke the intensity. I had to react to that—to the shooting of my wife, to the overall mission—all in a very compact, intense few moments. That's the kind of scene that an actor lives for."

One of the most internally discussed relationships in Season Five was between Bauer and his former lover Audrey Raines, played by Kim Raver. "Kiefer and I had a constant running dialogue about the relationship," says Raver. "We both knew that the connection between Jack and Audrey had to be solid and believable or a lot of the stuff going on around them would not be believable. That connection was what drew the audience in to the action, because the audience could care about them as people and not as just symbols."

Raver's favorite experience on *24* was filming the scene in which Bauer believes Raines to be a mole and so must interrogate her. "It was one of those acting days you really wait for," she says. "We were allowed to shoot just that scene for the whole day, which was unheard of. We were shooting about eight pages per day and this scene was just less than four pages. Jon [Cassar] and Kiefer both backed that because we all knew how important that scene was, how multi-layered it was, and that we had to successfully capture each layer. There was political stuff that we had to hit, relationship stuff, sexual tension, all kinds of stuff." Raver gives most of the credit for the success of the scene to Sutherland. "Kiefer is extraordinary to work with," she emphasizes. "In those moments you see the difference between Kiefer and other actors. When 'Action!' is called and you look into his eyes, he is right in it and that allowed me to get right in it as well."

Renowned character actor William Devane, who played the U.S secretary of defense for three seasons, also sings Sutherland's praises. "Kiefer is the ultimate pro," he says. "He sets a near perfect example when we're working. You can't wander too far off the path when you're working alongside a guy who works as hard as he does and contributes as much as he does."

Sutherland considers himself to be a normal guy. But his award for best actor in a dramatic series at the 2006 Emmys, for his work on Season Five, perhaps belies this perception. *24* won the Emmy for best dramatic series, and director Jon Cassar after accepting the prize for best director of a dramatic series, looked back at the evening: "I don't think there has ever been a night as exciting in my life. And the key to that was that we all won. If Kiefer hadn't won . . . it just would not have been the same, not as meaningful for any of us. But he did, as he deserved to, and it was the greatest night we could have hoped for."

By the end of Season Five, Sutherland had appeared in 120 hours of *24* and had made Jack Bauer a pop-culture icon. On April 10, 2006, it was announced that Sutherland and Fox Broadcasting had reached an agreement to extend his contract for another three full years. Reportedly, Sutherland would receive $40 million per season, but that figure was only for his acting chores; his participation in profits from the show, its syndication, DVD sales, and other ancillary monies made the contract even fatter still. Sutherland's official announcement in response to his deal was gracious: "The extraordinary support we have received from Fox has made a difficult show like *24* succeed on all levels, and for that I am truly grateful. I am thrilled to extend my commitment to all my friends and colleagues at *24,* and I'm looking forward to this expanded relationship with 20th Century Fox."

As part of the new deal, Sutherland was promoted from co-executive producer to executive producer, making him one of the senior bosses of the show. Sutherland was now more than a television star. He was an icon. The show had also imparted to his voice an undeniable weight of authority. When director Bruce Goodson was making his docudrama, *The Flight That Fought Back,* which recalled the fateful events aboard United Airlines Flight 93 on 9/11, he wanted Sutherland to do the voice-over narration to add the power and authority of Jack Bauer, even if subliminally, to the film.

When a reflective Sutherland looks back on the stellar Season Five, he has this to say about it: "I don't think this season was any more special than the others; I think there were very special things about the other seasons as well. It's just that I have learned more doing this show than from anything else I have ever done. When you go from film to film you can make broad creative choices from one project to another. This show has taught me about working with minutiae. I end up thinking about making fifteen small changes over the course of a season that end up making a huge difference."

Since its debut, *24* had become a lightning rod for the ongoing debate on national/homeland security, which was intensified by revelations of U.S.-sanctioned torture at Abu Ghraib prison in Iraq and at secret CIA detention sites around the world. By bringing these issues straight into American living rooms, *24* was inevitably drawn into the debate.

Sutherland was asked constantly about this angle of the show, especially when Season Six took the torture element one step further than real life, by having Bauer torture his own brother to near death. Sutherland feels torn. "What you have to remember is that this is a TV show," he says. "The torture sequences are done as a kind of dramatic device. Because the show is done in real time, the torture is used to illustrate the urgency of each moment." But he remains conflicted about the show's use of torture, even for purely dramatic reasons: "I have wrestled with that on this show . . . these characters and these situations and this world they are in, that is a world with different rules. But yes, I wrestle with those things constantly."

Personally, Sutherland is quite clear, he is against torture: "Not only don't I believe in torture as a way of gaining intelligence and information, I think it is probably the worst way in the world you can go about attempting to gain intelligence. Think of it, a person under that kind of duress and physical pain will naturally tell the torturer anything they thing they want to hear to make the pain stop. Even the toughest, best trained people will eventually talk under the right circumstances. It may take awhile longer, but every human being has to have a breaking point."

Creator and executive producer Joel Surnow is not entirely in agreement. On the wall behind his desk at the Real Time Productions offices, Surnow displays a framed, tattered American flag. It was given to him by a group of soldiers serving in Iraq in gratitude for Surnow arranging for a large shipment of *24* DVDs to the troops there for their entertainment. "The guys serving in Iraq love the show," says Surnow. "DVDs of the show are all over Iraq, wherever the guys are stationed. I think they love the show and love the Jack Bauer character because he is a patriot, first and foremost. He is selflessly serving his country, but he does it in the most non-bureaucratic of ways. Jack reacts to the situation; he gets things done with the sole purpose of saving Americans from external and internal threats."

Nevertheless, the program again ran into questions surrounding its depiction of torture. Although never attributed to a specific source, a comment circulated in the press claiming that cadets at the U.S. military academy at West Point were studying *24* to learn how to torture detainees. This became such an issue that the writing staff of *24* actually met with General Finnegan, the dean at West Point, to discuss this. General Finnegan wanted to make sure the writers knew that their show was not used as a teaching tool and that torture, as it was depicted in the show, was far from national policy. Likewise, the writers assured General Finnegan that they used torture simply to heighten tension. As writer Evan Katz says, "We put people in situations that would never happen in real life, so their methods of getting themselves out of those situations are also very much outside of reality."

As if the exertions of Season Five were too much, Season Six is clearly the weakest of the series. The character of Bauer changes dramatically. Released from a Chinese prison, he arrives home, not having spoken during almost two years in captivity. "It was the first time the character of Jack Bauer was truly indifferent," says Sutherland. "At the end of Season Five, Jack smiled briefly at Audrey; there was a sense that he felt he just might be able to get his life back. Then, after being captured, he realizes that he has lost everything: his relationship with his daughter, his new love, everything. That made him completely indifferent to everything, to life itself. That created a wonderful arc to create as an actor." Sutherland jumped into this personality change in Bauer. "Early in the season, Jack was doubting if he could continue this kind of life and work effectively, not by choice, but because of a fracturing of his psychological resolve," he says. "That was very interesting to play. It showed Jack not just to be flawed but also as a character that could be broken, a character that had limits just like everyone else; his limits are just broader and deeper than most."

Unfortunately for Sutherland, the improbability of the events in the season's storyline makes it seem more like an Irwin Allen disaster movie. It looked like the series had run out of steam; everything felt forced, and the plot twists were now so frequent that the credibility of all the characters was compromised. And while the regular cast performed well, a few new characters didn't work out at all.

The criticisms that Season Six received were not lost on the *24* production team. "This is a tough show to write," says writer Manny Coto. "It is a soap opera really, and because it is a soap opera we are bound by not just what came before us but by what we have to project that might happen several unwritten episodes down the road." The writers and the producers were now aware that they had pretty much run through the gamut of easily conceivable villains—Islamic extremists, Russian thugs, and Mexican narco-terrorists—so the challenges they faced for their next two seasons had to do with plausibility. "When we were all thinking of villains, we had to look further than where we had been looking," says writer Evan Katz. "There was a lot of talk about how the show had this right-wing agenda, but that is not true at all. Of the eight of us who write the show, only two of us are conservatives, and that includes creator Joel Surnow. When we look out the window at this time, the big villains out there are bloated corporations, big oil. We began thinking about making the connection between terrorism and corporate greed and avarice."

As preparations began for the seventh season of *24*, everyone connected with the show knew they had their work cut out for them. The grind was getting to all of them. "Making the show is tougher on the crew, I think," says Sutherland. "We have retained almost a hundred percent of our crew since we began, and that is almost unheard of in series television, over a six-year stint. For guys with families that is tough, because they don't get to see them hardly at all during shooting. For those that don't have families, it makes it tough to develop relationships or have a life outside of this show and this group of people."

On November 5, 2007, however, the Writers Guild of America went on strike, forcing the shutdown of production on all television shows and films involving its members. The seventh season of *24* had already started shooting; eight episodes, a third of the season, had been completed, and a debut date for Season Seven had been announced for January 13, 2008. Fox executives and the *24* team had to quickly decide what to do. They tried to make their decision based on what the fans of the show would expect rather than what worked for them in terms of convenience or expense. The final decision was announced by the Fox scheduling boss, Preston Blackman, after it became clear that the strike would be a long and divisive one: "The seventh season of *24* will be postponed immediately to ensure that the season can air uninterrupted, in its entirety." Blackman later commented that it was "not a decision anyone wanted to make, but it [was] one based on how we feel the fans expect us to react to this situation. The fans have shown us that they love following the season from start to finish. To begin airing under the present circumstances [would] allow us to begin, but who knows when we [would] ever get to the end."

The strike ended February 12, 2008, and according to Sutherland, it actually may have been a good thing for the show: "One of the positive by-products of the strike was that it freed us up;

it freed the writers up to really sketch out the season and actually write it fully so when we got back to shooting, we knew where we were going and where it was all ending up."

Sutherland was looking for ways to improve his faltering series. The original storyline for Season Seven had Jack Bauer in Africa, in Sangala, a fictional country torn by civil war. "The story set in Africa was interesting to me," says Sutherland. "I was thinking of what happened in Rwanda and the U.S. response, or lack of response, to what was happening there. I thought it was an interesting thing to have Jack Bauer involved in." As attractive as the African setting was, they knew from the shooting they had done before the WGA strike that there were problems to overcome. One was the time difference between the U.S. and Africa. Another was the expense of filming at African locations within the framework of a twenty-four-episode shoot.

As producer Howard Gordon explains, "We were struggling to do something new for this season. We were feeling the heat about everything always happening in L.A., so we sent Jack to Africa. The script that I wrote ended up not really working at all. Before the studio guys even saw the script it was looking like the Africa shoot would not fit in with our budget, both in terms of time and money. So we decided to scrap that storyline and retool the whole season in a very tight two weeks." In an echo of earlier times, the last-minute decision making came to a head at a meeting at none other than the same IHOP where they started, with Joel Surnow, Robert Cochran, and Howard Gordon.

When the WGA strike halted production on *24*, Season Seven was scheduled to recommence in July. But since the strike had, for all intents and purposes, caused the show to be delayed a full year, all of a sudden there was a budget for an Africa shoot. It was an opportunity to do something really bold and unique. Producers Surnow, Cochran, Sutherland, and Gordon came up with the idea to do a two-hour made-for-TV movie to bridge the gap between what happened in Season Six and what was about to happen in Season Seven. Howard Gordon would write the screenplay and Jon Cassar would direct the film, which for the time being, they entitled *24: Exile*.

"There was early talk about a feature-film version of *24* possibly going into production in 2007, for release in 2008," says Sutherland. "I always thought that the feature-film would be the grand finale, the end of the whole thing, but I am glad we went this route. It allowed us to go outside the format while still giving our audience what they love best about the show: smart, tense drama."

Surnow, Gordon, and Cassar headed to Cape Town, South Africa, to scout locations and look for local actors. The initial plan was to shoot on location in South Africa for just three days, then film the rest of the African scenes in a wooded area around Enola, Pennsylvania. But when the team started to scout South Africa and speak to people there, they knew that the African scenes needed to be filmed in Africa. "There is something about being there, in South Africa, something very unique," says Sutherland. "Johannesburg has to be one of the most dangerous cities on the face of the earth. There is desperate poverty in a place that also boasts a multi-billion-dollar diamond industry. We never would have been able to recapture the feel and the look and the atmosphere of the real place. The local dialects that people speak—we never could have replicated that. Shooting in Africa made that show what it was." The decision was made, and shooting began in South Africa in early June and went on for just over two weeks before the crew returned to Los Angeles for another month of filming.

24: Redemption was done in real time again, although this time the action covers two hours, from 3:00 p.m. to 5:00 p.m. in the afternoon. The film is an improvement over what audiences had last seen from the *24* team. Once again Sutherland delivers a splendid performance as a burned out Jack Bauer, who is trying to do penance in Africa but is drawn into a battle more fierce and brutal than any he has fought in before. Sutherland earned another Emmy nomination for his work, this time in the category of best actor in a made-for-TV movie.

His fondest memories of the *24: Redemption* shoot are of the young boys who played the children that his and Carlyle's character were sheltering from the violence of the war around them: "It was heartbreaking because these kids really didn't have much in their lives. But they were wonderful to work with, because they brought a purity of spirit to their work with us." Director Jon Cassar also became very close to the young South African boys; he spent hours with them explaining shots and scenes and motivation and helping them with lines. Sutherland remembers how hard it was to leave: "When Jon and I said good-bye to them, they cried. It was heartbreaking. They had grown close to us and we to them. Jon and I kept trying to figure out how we could take these boys with us and work them into the Season Seven storyline, anything rather than saying goodbye to these brave and spirited young men."

With *24: Redemption* in the can, it was time to get back to work on Season Seven. But for the first time in the series' history, writing had become a major problem. The original plan had been to begin shooting the episodes anew in July 2008, scrapping what had been filmed earlier. When scripts for the new direction of the show weren't ready, the date was pushed back to August. Shooting began but was then stopped again on August 27 for a couple of weeks, resuming only on September 10. "We really weren't sure about the storyline," says Howard Gordon. "So we shut down again for a couple of weeks to work on the next batch of scripts to make sure the storyline would hold."

In mid-September, production shut down yet again with just six episodes left to shoot. "We thought we had it," says Sutherland. "But we realized we didn't have a logical, satisfying conclusion to the season in place. So we shut down and retooled those last episodes to make sure the season ended strongly."

Season Seven was a watershed off-screen as well as on. After Season Six, several of the show's people had begun to feel that their creative juices were exhausted where *24* was concerned. Creator and producer Joel Surnow left the show halfway through the season saying, "I did some soul searching during the WGA strike, and I started working on some other things on my own, and I just felt that it was time to move on and stretch and try some things that were a bit outside of the mainstream." His co-creator Robert Cochran left at the end of the season. Even with series producer-writer Howard Gordon being promoted to fill Surnow's position, these departures left a sizable hole in the creative team. When director Jon Cassar announced he was stepping down as well, Brad Turner, who directed ten episodes of Season Seven, was promoted to co-executive producer and main director. Turner was not just a *24* veteran; he had done stellar work on another Fox hit as well, *Prison Break*.

"Working with Joel and Bob and especially Jon Cassar has been the longest and certainly the most creatively rewarding experience of my entire career," says Sutherland. "We developed a closeness that went far beyond just a working relationship, and that closeness built a trust that allowed the creativity to flourish to an even greater degree."

Fox Broadcasting President Gary Newman praised Sutherland for his continued commitment to the show and to Fox: "Shows like *24* go through changes throughout their run. The challenge is to replace strong talents with other strong talents. But with this show there is a comfort and a confidence because of Kiefer and his commitment to it. He is not just an actor on the show, he is a driving force for the entire team. With Kiefer and the more hands-on role that we have assigned Brad Turner, *24* is in good shape."

18

PERKS OF FAME

"We're kind of in our own cocoon making it. Every once and a while you stick your head up for a second, and you just can't believe how successful the show has become."

–Kiefer Sutherland

In 2002, Kiefer Sutherland was a Golden Globe-winning TV star with a hit show that was growing in the ratings almost weekly. Although his success did not affect him the way it often does others, it still forced him to change. Whereas he had been living from one movie location to another for years, he was now based in Los Angeles for at least ten months a year. He needed a permanent home.

Rather than buy a mansion in Beverly Hills like some new star trying to confirm his newly elevated status, Sutherland chose to settle on North Madison Avenue in a nondescript section of Los Angeles known as Silver Lake. He paid $700,000 for a 14,400-square-foot building, built in 1928, that was formerly an iron foundry. It is a huge, open structure that is mostly one large space. It consists of two levels: an upper level of 6,000 square feet and a lower level of 8,400 square feet. Sutherland lives upstairs. His living space has twenty-five-foot ceilings, four bathrooms and an open-concept living room. His sleeping area is set apart from the rest of the floor by a half wall. "It took me awhile to get used to sleeping in a barn," Sutherland remarks

Initially, he housed his beloved collection of vintage guitars here, a collection that has been valued at almost $180,000 and includes such beauties as a 1959 Les Paul, a 1967 Telecaster, a 1968 ES335, and at least fifty more. He later moved the collection downstairs to the offices of his music company.

Sutherland's surroundings are hardly upscale. "In my neighborhood the two major gangs are Salvadoran and Ukrainian. When I walk my dog at night, there are these guys hanging around who you know are serious gangbangers." Sutherland has been held up in that neighborhood, with a gun pressed to his head, on an occasion or two.

* * * *

Despite living in Los Angeles, a city virtually wedded to the automobile, Sutherland's preferred mode of transportation is the subway. While using public transportation might be thought to present problems for a well-known television star, he has his own logic for the choice. "Getting around on the subway allows you to have a few drinks when you're out," he says. He is recognizable, he acknowledges, but he adds, "In just about any situation, like in a bar or restaurant, when someone recognizes me I just say, 'Hi, how are you doing.' Once you do that they will say, 'I'm good, how are you doing?' And then I say, 'Good, man. Talk to you later.' And that is pretty much it." On occasion he is approached by a tough guy wanting to have a go at Jack Bauer. "That happens," says Sutherland,

"and it really depends on my mood. Catch me on a bad day when I feel I don't need that kind of thing, and whack!"

Despite the unruliness of his drinking, there is a surprising discipline to Sutherland's private life. His home is exceptionally tidy, especially for someone who lives alone. The cast of *24* once came over for dinner, and one-time girlfriend Reiko Aylesworth observed that it was nice of him to have cleaned up the big place for them. But he always keeps his place that neat: "I am a pretty demanding person," he says. "I like things to be a certain way, from being on time to being tidy. As I've gotten older, I hopefully have become a lot more flexible. But, of course, I am living alone."

Sutherland is obsessively neat. His packs of Camels are squared to the edges of the table. In his trailer on the set of *24*, scripts and magazines and books are all stacked in an orderly fashion; symmetry is always preserved. This fastidiousness stands in stark contrast to the personal disarray that Sutherland so often creates for himself in public. Another quirk is that Sutherland doesn't like to have mirrors in his homes. He has a mild phobia of them; the clinical term is *eisoptrophobia*. Some say that people who don't like mirrors around are not so much afraid to look *at* themselves but are afraid to look *into* themselves.

* * * *

In 2003, as Sutherland was settling into the life of a mega-star, he decided to venture into an area he has loved his whole life: music. "[Music] really dictates a lot about my life, how I view things and feel things," he says. "My whole mood or sense can change by virtue of the music I am listening to. It really does affect me on a visceral and emotional level."

But while other well-known actors have used their money to subsidize their rock 'n' roll fantasies, forming bands and recording albums, Sutherland has taken a different tack. "I'm [just] an okay musician," he says. "I try to take lessons as often as I can so I can improve, rather than just picking away at the same terrible thing over and over."

Instead of banging out songs himself, he channels his energy into creating opportunities for young up-and-coming bands and musicians. In 2003, he went into partnership with his longtime friend Jude Cole, a musician and record producer from Illinois. Sutherland had recorded a spoken word performance for the song "Joe from Cole's" on Cole's 1995 album *I Don't Know Why I Act This Way*. They christened their new record label Ironworks. "It is a label and a production company, and we do management as well," says Sutherland. "We look to launch new artists or to back artists who are having trouble establishing themselves in the larger corporate music world."

Sutherland doesn't do any of the producing himself; he allows the much more experienced Cole or other professional producers to handle that. "I am the guy who helps discover the acts, and I do a lot of the financing," he says. "We work in two facets. We either release a record on our own, through an independent distribution facility, or we shop the deal to a larger outfit like Warner or Universal, like we did with MoZella."

"I love music," he continues. "When I see a band that I think fits in with what we are trying to accomplish with the label, I'll approach Jude, and we'll get into a real dialogue on what to do about them." The first act that Ironworks signed was a folk-rock band called Rocco DeLuca and the Burden. Their first album, financed by Sutherland and produced by Cole, was called *I Trust You to Kill*

Me. Sutherland was so caught up with the band that he appointed himself tour manager for their first world tour and hired a crew to make a documentary of their journey. The documentary, which bears the same title as the album, is fascinating and shows Sutherland as a passionate, hard-working music professional who even goes out into the streets in places like Dublin, Ireland, to solicit fans and pass out free tickets. The documentary, which made a rousing debut at the Nashville Film Festival on April 22, 2006, follows the band from Los Angeles to London, Berlin, Dublin, and Reykjavik, Iceland.

Recent Ironworks signings have included the L.A. band Billy Boy on Poison, for their album *Drama Queen Junkie,* and the legendary Toronto-based folk musician Ron Sexsmith, a singer who has been praised by everyone from Bob Dylan to Chris Martin of Coldplay.

Sutherland literally keeps Ironworks close to home. He converted the lower level of his home, the 8,400 square feet of open space, into a full-service recording studio, complete with offices and lounges. He is pleased with what they have accomplished and by the loyalty of the groups he has worked with. "Even as people have found success in what they are doing, they have ended up staying because there is such a fantastic community here," he says. "And that has lent a great kind of vibe to the studio." Jude Cole confirms the sentiment: "For us it is all about getting really talented musicians to a place where they can get their music to the people. We are helping them find their way in what is becoming a very shrinking corporate music industry."

Sutherland details the pair's particular approach to their business. "As we were developing this facility and this concept, I wanted to make sure we had the money to do it," he explains. "I didn't want us to be in a position where we had to rent the studio out to cover expenses. I want the people here to be the people I want to have here. I don't want strangers wandering around. I want the people we are working with here to have a comfortable, cool environment to be in."

Creating and maintaining a comfortable atmosphere in a gang-controlled part of Los Angeles presented a few challenges. "To the north of us, it is all Salvadorans gangs. To the south is Ukrainian," Sutherland explains. "They do not ever cross into the other's territory, and they use our building as a giant memo pad for tagging [graffiti]. Every other day one gang will leave a message on our wall for another gang." Sutherland and company are not quick to paint over the graffiti. "No, we want to make sure that the other gang gets the message. We definitely don't want to get in the middle of things or cause anyone problems. But that said, generally the people in the neighborhood have been really good to us here. I would have a lot more problems trying to do this in Bel Air or Brentwood, I promise you."

* * * *

When Sutherland was shooting the documentary *I Trust You to Kill Me,* as he toured with his Ironworks band Rocco DeLuca and The Burden, he decided to get a new tattoo to commemorate the event. The documentary shows a guitar-strewn, grungy tattoo parlor in Reykjavik, Iceland, where Sutherland is sitting in a chair getting a large tattoo on the underside of his right forearm. The tattoo reads "I trust you to kill me," but is written in the Icelandic rune alphabet. Kiefer is clearly in a boozy, hazy state. His speech is slow and slightly slurred, as he alternately talks and grimaces from the pain. Someone off camera is asking him about his life and his attitude and why he is having those words inked onto his flesh. "I am going to do whatever

I want," he responds. "I am going to do whatever I think is right." The accented voice asks him if he cares what anyone thinks of him. "That's ridiculous. Of course I care what people think of me. But I've come to reckon with the idea that not everyone is going to like me, not everyone is going to like what I do." He goes on, "The times I have made the biggest mistakes as an actor were when I was trying to please everyone else and was not doing what my heart was telling me to do."

By now, Sutherland has many tattoos, beginning with the Chinese symbol for courage he got when he was just starting out as an actor. He has so many that it takes the make-up people at *24* quite a bit of time each day to cover them up. "Sometimes when I see myself without the tattoos on the set I think maybe I shouldn't have got any," he says. "But most of the time it is a nice map for myself of the journey of my life."

* * * *

A nice sideline for internationally recognizable Hollywood actors is doing foreign TV commercials. These jobs are paid exorbitantly well. During the 2007 production break on *24*, Sutherland accepted almost a million dollars for quick trip to Brazil to shoot a commercial for Citroën. During his brief stay in Rio de Janeiro Kiefer stayed at the legendary Copacabana Palace Hotel and was seen in the hotel's piano bar enjoying himself with a table full of beautiful Brazilian women. He was also paid a rumored $2.5 million to shoot a commercial for a Japanese drink called Calorie Mate. That commercial is a hilarious send up of *24*, with Sutherland as Jack Bauer, young Japanese girls as his operatives, and music that parodies the series. "When he was asked some time later by an American talk-show host why he does commercials, he shot back, "The question is, why wouldn't I?"

* * * *

24's production schedule does not allow Sutherland much time to do feature films; he can do perhaps one a year, if he is lucky. He often does voice work, though, which has become a lucrative career-within-a-career for him.

In 2004, Sutherland narrated an IMAX film called *NASCAR 3D,* which took audiences right inside the rip-roaring, paint-against-paint world of NASCAR auto racing. Explaining why he agreed to do this project, he says, "It's a real slice of Americana. It's birth during the time of prohibition gives this sport a very particular authenticity—guys muscling up cars so they could run moonshine on back roads while outrunning the police."

Sutherland attended a couple of races to get the feel of the sport and came away impressed. "These drivers are incredibly disciplined and focused guys," he says. "They joke around with their pit crews and enjoy real interaction with their fans, but fifteen minutes later, when they climb into their cars, there is a transformation you can see in their faces and their body language. They become gladiators. They're roaring around in these monster cars taking corners at 200 mph while banging into each other. It's amazing, very exciting."

Besides voice-overs, animation work is a lucrative aside and a great love of his. Asked about his relationship to animated films in general, he speaks from the heart: "I remember seeing *Bambi* as a kid, and I just felt very strongly about that deer. It moved me so much, when the mother got killed and all that." He goes on in a serious tone, "Bambi really had to struggle growing up. I guess I must have seen that movie at seven or eight times. Cinderella was more designed for my sister to enjoy. But as a guy, I felt okay about feeling what I felt for that little animal." Sutherland got to take his own place in the world of Disney animation when in 2005, he did the voice for the main character, a young lion, in the Disney animated film *The Wild*, "a father and son story really," he says.

When Jeffrey Katzenberg was putting together his ambitious film, 2009's *Monsters vs. Aliens*, an animated film in which the director was trying to push the cinematic use of 3-D technology to the next level, he specifically wanted Sutherland for the voice of one of the characters. "Kiefer has a voice that is perfect for animated films," says Katzenberg. "It's a voice that is both authoritative and soothing, depending on the requirement of the role." The problem was finding time to fit the film into his *24* schedule. "That ended up not being a problem at all," says Sutherland. "Doing these kinds of animated films is a very liberating thing for an actor to do. You're using only your voice, so you can do whatever you need to physically to get the line reading right. The physicality means nothing, and so the process is fantastic. I would do my scenes for five or six hours over a couple of weekends, in between shooting episodes of *24*."

"There were a couple of reasons that I wanted to be a part of this film," he elaborates. "I love those old, over-the-top horror films like *Godzilla* and *King Kong*, the campy one with Jeff Bridges and Jessica Lange. But really I did the film simply for the message: that not only is it alright to be different, but what makes you different can be the best thing about you."

* * * *

Although Sutherland has lived in Los Angeles most of his adult life, with pockets of time spent in the Santa Ynez Valley and Montana, he still refers to Toronto as his hometown. He visits there frequently. "I own a house in Toronto, but whenever I go there I tend to stay at the Windsor Arms Hotel," he says. The Windsor Arms is a legend among midtown hotels. In the 1960s Elizabeth Taylor and Richard Burton kept a suite on perpetual reservation just for them. The Hotel fell into disrepair in the 1970s and was restored to its former luxury in the early 1990s. "I love the minimalist feel of the suites there," Sutherland says. "They kind of remind me of the apartment Mickey Rourke had in *9½ Weeks*."

Another draw that the Windsor Arms has for Sutherland is its restaurant, The Courtyard Café. "[It has] literally the best mushroom soup in the entire world; it's like taking regular mushroom soup and sending it through a puree—phenomenal taste and very light." In fact, Sutherland is something of a connoisseur of Toronto's eateries. A short walk from the Windsor Arms is Flo's, the place where Sutherland always has breakfast when in town. "It's a real diner-looking diner, not a faux diner. This place is what a diner should look like," Sutherland insists. And as he does in Los Angeles, when he is in Toronto, Sutherland likes to travel around on the subway. "There are a couple of areas I like to just walk around in," he says. "I love walking about The Annex [a part of town that can be likened to Greenwich Village in New York City], and I love going to the Danforth section, the Greek part of town, where two of my favorite Greek restaurants in the world are, Christina's and Myth."

On the more upscale side is Bistro 990, a place where he often takes his mother for dinner when they are both in town. "I love Bistro 990 for a couple of reasons," he says. "They have a great bar in the basement, and the restaurant is like an old German place—real arches and low ceilings, a great atmosphere. I remember eating there a number of times with Jon Cassar [the director of 24] who is also from Toronto and also knows it well."

Another place Sutherland frequents when in Toronto is the Avenue Bar at the Four Seasons Hotel. The Four Seasons Hotel is where most Hollywood folks stay when working or playing in Toronto. "It is amazing there," Sutherland remarks. "I used to joke around that the Avenue Bar at the Four Seasons in Toronto was the hottest bar in Hollywood. But it really isn't a joke anymore. I run into more of my L.A. friends there than I do in L.A.!"

Every year, a celebration is held in Toronto's entertainment district, at the Canadian Walk of Fame. It is modeled after the more famous version on Hollywood Boulevard in Los Angeles. The Canadian Walk of Fame honors renowned Canadians with a granite plaque on the sidewalk in front of the Princess of Wales Theatre. On June 5, 2005, it was Sutherland's turn to receive his plaque; following the one awarded his father in 2000 and his mother in 2004.

It wasn't until December 9, 2008, that Sutherland got his star on the Hollywood Walk of Fame. Most of the cast and crew of *24* turned up, as did his father, his daughter, and one of his half brothers. Donald Sutherland proudly introduced his son, and when Kiefer took the stage he thanked his family and colleagues before profusely thanking 20th Century Fox, which had sponsored his induction to the Walk of Fame. Then he told the crowd of his early days of sleeping at the beach in his car, and that when he could afford a small Hollywood apartment, it was less than two blocks from where his star on sidewalk now was. After the ceremony, Sutherland and his father signed autographs and posed for pictures with fans. Speaking to a reporter at the event, Sutherland described his mood. "I used to walk up and down this street and look at the names. I remember Randolph Scott and Gary Cooper particularly: two guys who had rough starts to their careers as well, but here there are. I never dreamed I would ever be here with them."

****

The success of *24* has given Sutherland more recognition that he could ever have imagined. In 2006, he was named the fourth most powerful Canadian living in America by *Canadian Business* magazine, and in the same year *Forbes* magazine listed him at number sixty-eight on the top one hundred most powerful celebrities list. "I don't really pay much attention to that stuff," he says. "It is all just perception anyway, like the art world. One day a painting is worth a hundred thousand and a year from now it might be worth ten million. It is still the same painting; the perception has just changed."

Although he has received no shortage of media attention, Sutherland's relationship with the press, especially the paparazzi-driven tabloids, has always been fairly even. Unlike his friend Sean Penn, who used to love to slug photographers, Sutherland has allowed them to do their jobs while he did his. There have been exceptions. At his arrest for DUI, reporters and fans had gathered around his car to snap his picture with cameras and cell phones. A number of the photos ended up on the Internet. For months afterward, when someone tried to take his picture, Sutherland would turn away and say, "Nope, none of that. You guys screwed me." In 1993, Sutherland even sued one tabloid, *News of the World,* after the paper had published a story saying that his marriage to Camelia Kath was nothing but a publicity stunt. He won an apology and an undisclosed sum of money.

But Sutherland accepts the burden of celebrity, though, and approaches his interactions with the public with equanimity. One thing that often puts him in direct contact with his fans is smoking. "You cannot smoke anywhere indoors in L.A.," he notes. "So I have to go outside on the sidewalk to smoke. When I'm standing around smoking, people will notice me, smile at me, and hand me a pen and paper. I always try to sign my name clearly, no scribbling."

It is always a curiosity when stars who have gotten rich by being in the public eye profess to be uncomfortable when being recognized. Sutherland is not like that. "I like people. I know that the fans are the people who pay the money to see what I do," he says. "I know that without them I would be nothing. I just don't want to disappoint anyone."

19

SON AND FATHER

"The most significant piece of advice my father gave me early on about acting was 'Don't get caught acting.' He said to really believe in what you are doing and then commit to it—even if it's uncomfortable, even if you feel it will make you look like an ass. It's all acting, but find the truth in the moment rather than just pretending you have and rather than trying to act your way out of it."

–Kiefer Sutherland

When Sutherland talks about his father, he talks as though about an older friend he greatly admires. But when he talks about his mother, it is with a deference you expect from a son talking about a parent. "She is very smart," he says. "She is a very tough and very committed lady. She has been awarded the Order of Canada, the highest civilian medal you can get in Canada. She is five foot two, and I'll be honest with you, she is the only person I'm scared of."

Shirley Douglas raised Kiefer, of course, and dealt first-hand with the ups and down of his adolescence while Donald was far away in Los

Angeles. In the years since Sutherland's Hollywood career took off, however, the situation has reversed. Because Sutherland lives in L.A., he now sees more of his father. He still tries to visit his mother as much as he can in Toronto, where Douglas lives in a house Sutherland bought for her. But he seldom stays there with her when he is in town. "No room service," she explains.

They have reconnected as professionals a couple of times, but the parent-child relationship always rears its head. When Sutherland was working with his mother in 1997 on *The Glass Menagerie,* he described the experience this way: "It was pretty surreal at the time. When we were rehearsing we would be two professionals working; we were respectful and interacted as two members of the same team. But once we broke for lunch or wrapped for the day, she would go back to being my mother. Even the tone of her voice changed back to motherly and authoritative."

In 2008, they teamed again in brief cameos for the wildly successful Canadian sitcom called *Corner Gas,* which is set in Douglas's home province of Saskatchewan. In that episode, one of the characters is calling around frantically looking for help from local sports coaches. He calls a wrong number, and Sutherland answers the phone in a dimly lit room, where he is sitting in front of a computer. "We have a problem," says the caller. "We need to set up a perimeter." Jack Bauer's raspy voice responds, "Who is this?" "You're not the coach of the baseball team?" comes the puzzled reply. Sutherland tells the caller he has the wrong number and that he has reached Shirley Douglas's residence. "Are you sure?" the caller asks. "Yes, I should know. She's my mother," Sutherland responds. "You still live with your mother?" Sutherland's face grows dark, and he responds, "I'm hanging up now." The cameo finishes with Shirley Douglas calling from off camera, "Kiefer, who was that?" To which he snaps, "Damn it, mom. I told you to knock before you come in!"

* * * *

Kiefer Sutherland's relationship with his father Donald has long been a complicated one. From the moment they arrived in Hollywood from London, Donald and Kiefer were close, but distance has often foiled their relationship. "When we first arrived in Los Angeles from London, where I had been working, the U.S. customs guy asked me how long we planned to be in the country," the elder Sutherland relates. "I told the guy we were planning on staying perhaps six months or so. At that moment Kiefer cried out for all to hear, 'But you said we were going to stay here forever!' "

Kiefer's early memories of his Hollywood-movie-star father were indicative of the times and the place they were living in. "I remember little things," he says, "like being dropped off at day care when I was about four years old. My father's hair was long and flowing, and he had a full beard. He was wearing a big suede coat, and we were riding in a convertible sports car that he had won the night before in a card game."

The younger man has been asked a number of times if the Sutherland name opened Hollywood doors for him: "I have no way of knowing. This is my last name. If it opened doors, it opened doors. I didn't notice it all that profoundly. I can tell you that the name closed some doors on me early on, though. A lot of casting directors early in my career were wary of me being another second-generation actor trying to coast in on his parent's reputation."

Later though, when Sutherland got to know his father as a man, he became more descriptive in his thoughts and feelings about him. "Look at my father," he says. "He came from a small fishing village of five hundred people. He was six foot four, with giant ears and a very odd expression, and he thought he could be a movie star. If you see pictures of him at eighteen or nineteen you will not see a Robert Redford or Paul Newman type. Yet he still had the effrontery to go to England and pursue that dream. That is an amazing thing."

Donald Sutherland is, of course, very proud of his son Kiefer; his son's staggering success with *24* only deepened that pride and respect. Their relationship would get a boost in the spring of 2007, when Donald was cast in a regular role in the ABC TV series *Dirty Sexy Money*, which ran from September 2007 through August 2009. Though set in New York, it was filmed in L.A. "Once he got that role and was living in Los Angeles again, it gave us the chance to spend a lot more time together," says his son. "We started having dinner together regularly, getting together on Sundays, and spending time together at the beach just walking and conversing."

****

His disappointment about not having had as much time with his dad as he would have liked has caused Sutherland to reflect on the time he has missed with his own daughter, Sarah Jude. "Regret is not something I think is the least bit productive, so I try not to engage in it," he says "But I do regret not spending more time with my daughter. When that time is gone, it is gone. All that is left is trying to make up for the lost time by being as attentive and loving as you possibly can when you do spend time together."

Sutherland traces his longing for time lost with his own father back to when he was just thirteen, when he saw the emotionally powerful film *Ordinary People*, in which his father Donald starred. This film about family bonding and dealing with suicide won Oscars for both director Robert Redford and young co-star Timothy

Hutton. "There is a pivotal scene in the film, where the boy and his father are sitting and talking on the porch, and it is just beautiful," says Sutherland. "I remember thinking to myself, 'I would like to have that conversation with my dad.' That film also made me think, I guess I'm partially responsible; I have to instigate conversations too. "That film broke my heart, but it also opened my eyes."

It can be said that one of the reasons Sutherland ended up as Jack Bauer was a bi-product of this reflection. "That is absolutely true," confirms Sutherland. "My whole career, and my daughter's whole life, had seen me going from one film to the next, shooting all over the world. Having this series [*24*] meant that I would be in the same place at least eight months of the year."

Part of building a closeness with his daughter is getting to know what makes her tick. "I grew up listening to Canadian rock and roll, like Rush, and I loved listening to AC/DC and Bad Company," Sutherland admits. "My daughter listens to the music of her time: pop music and hip hop." In 2001, when she was thirteen, Sutherland took Sarah Jude to an Incubus concert, and he was surprised by her reaction to it: "She screamed in a way I never knew she had in her; she got wildly into the music. That was a wake-up call."

During his years on *24*, Sutherland has been committed to being present for her not just physically but emotionally as well. Part of his challenge in parenting is that he remembers how wild and rebellious he himself was. "As a parent you have to almost embrace that rebellion in your child," he says. "You have to remember, as a parent, what you were like as a teenager. They have so much energy. You have to embrace their desires, and their desires are, in all fairness, still pretty good and healthy." But if there is one thing he has trepidations about, it is answering the tough questions of life that teens have. "I just hope that I am smart enough with my daughter to understand, when those questions come up, what they really mean."

Sutherland gave his own mother a turn when he was just twelve years old, showing up at home with his head shaved and his ear pierced. For him it was just a natural rebellion. But when time circled around and his fifteen-year-old stepdaughter came home with the declaration that she wanted to shave her head, both her father and her mother, Camelia Kath, vehemently objected. Undaunted, she went out and shaved the underside of her head so the shaved part would be covered when her hair was down. When she was out with her friends, she would tie her hair up in a pony tail to expose the shaved part. "I had to act like I was mad at her," says Sutherland. "But part of me was very proud of her. She made it work for herself. Body piercing, tattoos, that is all the rage. Kids want to make their mark and identify themselves as part of their generation. It is healthy that they have to fight with their parents for it. It costs them something."

Sutherland has gone so far as to involve Sarah Jude in the family business. When she was sixteen, he got her a job as a production assistant on *24*. It took her a while to learn the ropes. "One of the things that I am very specific about on our show is that it has to be absolutely quiet," Sutherland explains. During one particularly tense take, when the cast was shooting on the second floor of the soundstage and all the production assistants were on the first floor keeping everyone quiet, a female voice suddenly yelled, "Rolling!" and ruined the take. Sutherland bellowed out, "Who the fuck!?" Then, more softly, "That was my daughter, wasn't it?" He had made it clear that his daughter was not to be shown any special consideration. "We found her a different job," he says now about the incident.

Her gaff hasn't stopped Sarah Jude from proudly trying to follow in her dad's footsteps. She has expressed to him a desire to try acting herself. "I can tell her that it is a million-to-one shot to be successful in show business," he says. "But what I cannot and will not do is discourage her from trying something she wants to do." He also says, like any proud father, "She's pretty clever; I'm very impressed by her. She has done her first play, and she is playing music in a band. I'm excited to see where this goes." And then as he often does, he analyzes his feelings about it a but more closely. "It actually took me a while to deal with the fact that she wants to do this," he admits. "I can't figure out whether it is my own ego that is saying 'This is what I do,' or if it's a parental fear saying, 'Please, baby, you don't want to do this; there is nothing but heartbreak.' "

Sutherland's marriage to Sarah Jude's mother Camelia Kath was a strange and rocky one. "For the longest time, Camelia thought I was quite a bit older than I was," says Sutherland. "Then, when I told her my real age and she found out I was more than a decade younger than her, it was a little late for her to do much about it."

Sarah Jude came along just a year into their marriage, and then the fact that he was really too young and emotionally immature for fatherhood hit home. "I feel horrible about this, but I remember at the time thinking, 'Oh God, if I have to go to the park one more fucking time and sit in a sandbox, I am going to lose my fucking mind' "

Sarah Jude has always been able to reduce her father to an emotional heap. Sutherland remembers one incident in particular that chokes him up every time he relates it. "I was having a bad day, and it was my fault," he recalls. "I picked my daughter up at school, and I remember just swearing at myself in front of her. I said something like, 'Fuck, I am such an asshole!' I looked back at her, and she was in shock. I told her that I was very sorry and sometimes I swore a lot but that was nothing to be proud of and she should not do it. Then she said, 'You could never be that, Daddy.' It just killed me."

"In a funny way, over the years, when Sarah was older and we had reconnected, it was almost like we were raising each other," Sutherland says. He recounts how his daughter, then a young teenager, came to him for his help in getting over the break-up with her first-ever boyfriend. "I didn't belittle the fact that she was really hurting, because she was really in love," he says. "She was fifteen, but I don't think there is an age when all of a sudden you feel that."

Sutherland took her to one of his favorite haunts, the Village Café in Beachwood Canyon, a place where he hung out and got wild with friends when he first hit Hollywood as a teenager. "I used to go there when I was sixteen," says Sutherland. "That was before I had children, before things became very important. We lived then with an ease that we thought was going to be with us all the time."

* * * *

Whenever he is asked about being a father, Sutherland becomes animated and effusive. "I could talk about that forever," he says. "From the fear of it, to the joy of it, to how much it made me laugh. I was twenty years old when I had a child, and I was too young. I remember apologizing to my daughter when she was about fourteen. She said, 'Dad, it's all right. I wouldn't have wanted it any other way,' I was so moved, I just lost it right there outside of Hamburger Hamlet."

Sutherland has always agonized over his relationship with his daughter, as many a father does. "It took me a very long time to realize I needed to be a responsible father and make her a major part of my life," he affirms. "I learn new, amazing things about her every day. Once she made a ceramic cup for me, and I realized that she had a grasp of irony when she wrote on it, 'My Daddy is a saint.' Obviously, she was joking."

20

WILD AND CRAZY

"I know I should be able to wake up in the morning without going, 'Oh, no! Where's my boot?' or 'Where am I?' or 'One of your friends didn't happen to bring my car home, did they?' It's not a clever way to live, and I don't want to live like that. But it's the kind of trade you have to make."

–Kiefer Sutherland

Despite the ten-month-a-year schedule, and frequent twelve-hour days on the set, being committed to *24* did not temper Sutherland's penchant for excessive drinking and partying. If anything it may have encouraged more of it, as he felt an increased need to let off steam from the pressure cooker of the heavy schedule and the relentless emotional intensity that was necessary to maintain for the screen.

One of the most fascinating things about Sutherland's behavior when he is away from the set, misbehaving and drinking to wild excess, is that he is unapologetic about it. Yes, he has made public apologies to his family and co-workers when his indiscretions have ended up all over the news, and he has undoubtedly made many private apologies to his daughter, stepdaughter and stepsons, and his colleagues as well. But he never issues disingenuous statements that he is changing his ways and seeking help for his problems. Kiefer Sutherland never does that. If he is called to defend himself, he shrugs, smiles his famous sheepish smile, and moves on.

His attitude doesn't come without its price, however. Sutherland carries around a chunk of broken glass in his elbow because of one such encounter with a couple of U.S. servicemen. He decided to take both of them on and confesses, "I got my ass kicked." He remembers rolling around on a floor where there was broken glass but didn't notice anything until he was X-rayed for a broken wrist from another fight. The X-ray detected a mass in his elbow, which turned out to be the piece of glass. "The doctor wanted to open my elbow to remove it, but I said, 'No, it's fine. Just leave it in there.' "

* * * *

At the after-party for the Golden Globes in 2002, Sutherland, still in shock from his win, was approached by a man who proclaimed himself a big fan of the show and of Sutherland. The man was Hugh Hefner. As the two talked, Sutherland mentioned that he had never been invited to the Playboy Mansion. Hefner immediately promised to correct that error, and Sutherland was duly invited to a pajama party at the mansion less than a month later.

Sutherland attended the party with one of his drinking buddies—most single, unattached Hollywood men go to a Hugh Hefner party alone or with a male friend, because they know what is waiting for them when they get there. Sutherland's only public commentary on that night was related to the place's exterior: "The Mansion had a huge yard, the biggest yard I had ever seen." But another actor, a Hefner-party regular, reveals that Sutherland got roaring drunk and sat at tables with other men or with some of the party girls there, saying loudly, "I'm in the Playboy Mansion. This is the fucking Playboy Mansion!" He was overwhelmed, perhaps, by all the controlled decadence going on around him. "I don't know if he seriously hooked up with anyone," adds the actor. "But he did disappear a couple of times with women and come back to the party looking a bit flushed and red in the face."

* * * *

A frequent drinking buddy of his relates that Sutherland's drinking was sometimes so out of control that his friends feared for his safety, "We would get together, often by accident. I would run into Kiefer and a friend in a bar or hotel lounge, and all of a sudden we would be drinking like fish together for hours. Kiefer would bang back J&B and coke hand over fist. Kiefer always does some fool-ass thing to make us all laugh. One time he just pulled his pants down around his ankles and sat there bare-assed to just see the kinds of reactions he would get from the people around him. Most just laughed, but one drunken woman came over and offered to blow him right there in the bar."

* * * *

By early 2004, Sutherland's drinking binges were not just legendary, they were a worry for the *24* team and the studio, 20th Century Fox. Occasionally, his employers were obliged to deal with the consequences of his benders. In January 2004, Sutherland was at a bar where he often went to relax after a series of shooting days and where he is known to drink until the place closes. On this night, he got into a drunken brawl and fought with several other men, breaking furniture and glassware and ending up with his face slashed by a broken glass. It took six stitches to close the gash. The bartender insists, "Kiefer did not start this fight; he was only defending himself."

While production of *24* didn't have to be delayed because of the incident, the shooting schedule had to be hastily rearranged to allow Sutherland's face time to heal. On his own initiative, Sutherland assembled the cast and crew on the set so he could apologize to them all for the disruption.

Then, in early April of 2004, a particularly embarrassing incident occurred that the studio tried to contain. On this spring morning, a restless Sutherland had begun drinking Scotch at 9:00 a.m in a gay bar on Santa Monica Blvd. At 1:00 p.m., after drinking for four hours, Sutherland stumbled out into the sunlight. A film was shooting across the street, and when its cast and crew members spied Sutherland a number of them asked him to pose for pictures. One of the crew members describes the scene: "He just reeked of booze and cigarette smoke, but he was happy and laughing. He could barely stand up, and when someone posed with him for picture he would literally fall against them." Sutherland then became Kiefer the Drunk Entertainer again. The crew member continued, "A girl from the crew tugged her jeans down over her ass to show Kiefer a tattoo she had on it. Kiefer then told her he had something to show her, and he pulled down his pants and showed everyone his ass."

Throughout 2004, reports surfaced almost weekly that Sutherland was drinking Scotch at bars around his home until 2:00 a.m., at which time he would then head to the closest after-hours bar and continue to binge until the early morning hours. When reporters asked studio executives to comment on their star's growing erratic behavior, the answer was always the same: Kiefer Sutherland had never been late for work and was never anything but completely professional on the *24* set.

Sutherland did not confine his antics to Los Angeles. In the summer of 2004, he was filming *The River Queen* in the town of Raetihi, on New Zealand's North Island. As he was heading back to his hotel after a booze-up, he heard some loud party music coming from a doorway and decided to go inside. It turned out to be a Chippendale's-style male strip revue in full swing, where a couple of hundred Kiwi women were hooting and hollering at a handful of male dancers. Though very drunk, Sutherland jumped up on stage and began stripping and gyrating as best he could to the song "You Can Keep Your Hat On." The crowd, recognizing him, egged him on. Encouraged, he then jumped down into the crowd of women and gave a couple of them rather unskilled lap dances before being good naturedly escorted from the premises.

* * * *

Inevitably, Sutherland started to experience the consequences of his behavior. In early November 2004, after a night of drinking and partying, Sutherland was driving home when he was pulled over by the LAPD for erratic driving. He was wobbly when he got out of his car and was promptly given a field sobriety test. His blood-alcohol level was 0.22. At this level there is characteristically stupor, loss of understanding, memory blackout, and severe motor impairment. Sutherland was charged with driving under the influence of alcohol. In court, he pleaded no contest and was placed on five years' probation. The presiding judge, the Honorable Michael Sauer, suggested it would be a good idea for the actor to seek treatment for his problem with alcohol. Sutherland did not take Judge Sauer's advice.

* * * *

As *24* brought more and more success for Sutherland, he found himself going from relationship to relationship. He has said in interviews that he is not a fan of one-night stands: "I have had them, but I like more of a connection—an intellectual connection, an emotional connection. One-night stands are akin to masturbation; it is a function, but it isn't really satisfying." Nevertheless, during the shooting of *24*, especially the first three seasons, Sutherland was reported to have had short-term affairs with several women who worked for or on the show. He says, "Love is a self-manifested notion that depends on how lonely you are. If you are really attracted to someone, and you are already lonely, I think you can fall in love in an instant. It is all about where you are at."

According to a young Canadian actress he dated during this time, "Kiefer is a wonderful guy, very sensitive and caring. Because he was working such long hours he really didn't have much time. He told me that he wasn't promising me anything. He just said, 'Let's see what happens.' " The pair would meet and enjoy dinner together, and sometimes they would they would steal away to a night together at a hotel. On one occasion, she says, "Kiefer took me back to his house. It was wonderful. He made me dinner and then we relaxed and he played one of his guitars. Then we left early the next morning."

Sutherland was rumored to be dating *24* co-star Reiko Aylesworth off and on between 2003 and 2005. Over Christmas in 2004, however, he met twenty-three-old model Kristin Haraldsdottir in Reykjavik, Iceland. They began to date. In April 2005, Haraldsdottir was quoted as saying, "There is a really good feeling between us. He is down to earth and a great guy and a lot of fun to be with." But by the middle of summer, he had moved on. Then in Toronto, shooting *The Sentinel* during the break in *24*'s production schedule, Sutherland became involved with one of his co-stars, *Desperate Housewives*' Eva Longoria. According to one of the makeup people on *The Sentinel*, Sutherland and Longoria were "the talk of the set because they were spending lots of time together hanging out in either his trailer or hers." The two were seen together several times in Toronto and Los Angeles, but eventually someone from Longoria's camp said publicly that "Kiefer and Eva are both really busy at the moment so they are taking it slowly." It was a clear sign that the romance had cooled.

When asked about his emotional state at this time, Sutherland said, "Breaking up has never been a strong suit of mine. I kind of start behaving as badly as possible until someone else will do it for me. And I regret that. The best you can do is find those people and say, 'Look, I haven't talked to you in a while, but I just wanted to say that I didn't like the way I treated you at that point; you didn't deserve that.' Yes, there are a few people in my life I would like to do that with."

* * * *

Despite his introspective insights after the fact, Sutherland's lack of good judgment is sometimes astonishing. In 2006, a report got back to him that U.S. college students who were hooked on *24* actually had created a frat-house drinking game to be played as the watched the show. The rules were simple: every time Jack Bauer uttered "Damn it!" the students had to quickly down a shot. Sutherland has toyed with them, ad libbing several of the curses during taping. In one episode, he says it three times in rapid succession; in another, fourteen times. "I could just see all these college kids going, 'Ah fuck!' " he says.

* * * *

Of all his notorious acts of buffoonery under the influence of alcohol, the Christmas-tree-tackling incident is probably the most spectacular. The critical moment was caught on video and posted on Youtube for the world to see. Sutherland tries to play down what happened, but two reporters were there to see it all unfold.

The London *Sunday Mirror*'s Emily Miller and Michael Duffy were covering Sutherland's arrival in town with singer Rocco Deluca, whom Sutherland was managing for his music company, Ironworks. The reporters were to meet up with him at the London club Borderline, where Deluca had his gig. When Sutherland came into the club, he literally ran into Miller, almost knocking her over. It was an accident, and Sutherland showered her with a litany of "I'm so sorry, I'm so sorry."

After the band played their gig, a performance met with only polite applause, Miller and Duffy joined Sutherland and the band members in the bar at the Strand Palace, a modest West End hotel. There, "the drinking REALLY began," writes Duffy. Sutherland established a tab in his name and ordered "tray after tray of whisky, beer, gin, and wine." By this time, Sutherland was completely hammered. He pulled Miller over to show her the Icelandic rune tattoo on his forearm. "Sit down and take a look at this," he slurred. "It says, 'I trust you to kill me.' It's the name of Rocco's new album. To me it also means, 'Fuck you!' There is a lot of disrespect bound up in it."

At 2:00 a.m., the bar staff refused to serve any more alcohol to them. Sutherland was not to be denied, however, and convinced the night-management staff to allow him to order more booze from room service and take the party to the lobby. Sutherland was now falling-down drunk and tried to get laughs from his party by doing a strange, uncoordinated break-dance routine.

Then he saw the Christmas tree. Sutherland bellowed, "I hate that fucking Christmas tree. The tree has to come down." He then staggered around addressing the staff, "I'm smashing it. Can I pay you for it?" To which one staff member replied, "I'm absolutely sure you can, sir."

Sutherland got ready, then he launched himself into the decorated Norwegian spruce, sending its lights, tinsel, and glass balls flying everywhere. After wrestling the tree to the ground, Sutherland got up, pulling pine needles out of his clothing and his hair. He staggered to the hotel staffer saying, "Oh, sorry about that . . . you are so cool. This fucking hotel rocks!"

One of the band members tried to urge Sutherland to head to his room and call it a night, but Sutherland shook off his friend and staggered toward the two *Sunday Mirror* reporters. He grabbed Michael Duffy's hand and shook it with great animation. He then started to cry as he described how disappointed he was at the poor reaction to the band. "It was bollocks," he said. "We've played a lot of other places, and they went nuts for this shit." Almost incoherently, he addes, "In this world you have to share something with the fucking band." He then playfully called Duffy, who is from Down Under, a "fucking Aussie cunt" before kissing him on the head. Sutherland turned his attention to Miller, holding her hand and drunkenly stroking her shoulder. He leaned toward her, telling her, "Don't go, don't go; I have a crush on you." Gently rebuffed by Miller, Sutherland proceeded to stumble down the eighth-floor hallway of the hotel searching for his room. He eventually found the door that fit his key and disappeared inside.

21

JAIL

"Doing the time was probably the easiest part. The embarrassment I caused my family, my daughter, and my colleagues, that was the tough part. That said, I am not looking to repeat the experience any time soon."

–Kiefer Sutherland

On September 24, 2007, Fox hosted their annual Fox Fall Eco-Casino at the trendy West Hollywood club Area. The charity casino night featured Fox stars and executives playing table games, drinking, and having fun, with the proceeds going to Habitat for Humanity and the Nature Conservancy. Sutherland was in attendance, enjoying the evening with drinks, friends, and colleagues. He left the club shortly after 1:00 a.m. While driving through West Hollywood he thought he would take a shortcut and made a U-turn. In a stroke of misfortune, he executed his haphazard maneuver right in front of an LAPD patrol car. Sutherland was pulled over and asked if he had been drinking. He admitted that he had been, a little bit. In an all-too-familiar scenario, LAPD officers gave him a field sobriety test and made him blow into a Breathalyzer. He reportedly came in just over twice California's legal limit of 0.08. Sutherland was taken into custody and driven to the Hollywood police station. At 4:00 a.m. he was formally charged with driving under the influence. His mug shots and fingerprints were taken, and at 5:42 a.m. he was released on a $25,000 bond. At a hearing on September 28, he was formally charged both with DUI and with violating the conditions of the probation order from his last DUI conviction in 2004.

Shortly after he was released from LAPD custody, and just as the story of his arrest was hitting the airwaves, Sutherland presented himself at the Los Angeles residence of the Canadian Consul General. Sutherland was there to get the ACTRA (Alliance of Canadian Cinema, Television and Radio Artists—the Canadian version of the American Screen Actors Guild) Award of Excellence from Consul General Alain Dudoit and ACTRA president Richard Hardacre. A somber but polite and smiling Sutherland accepted the award graciously after being praised by Dudoit: "We are proud to present this award to Kiefer Sutherland, who, as a Canadian working in the U.S., has built one of the most successful careers in Hollywood." Richard Hardacre then added, "It is an honor to recognize him not only for his unique work, but for his strong support to his fellow Canadian actors working in Los Angeles."

Interviewed later, Hardacre addressed the unfortunate timing of the event: "We had planned the event for a long time," he says. "And while the DUI thing was embarrassing and unfortunate, Kiefer took the hit like a man. It did nothing to diminish the fact that Kiefer is a pro; he is a Canadian who helps many, many Canadians in Hollywood. Look at *24;* every season has at least a dozen Canadians in front of and behind the camera. There are some American shows shot in Canada that don't even have that."

On October 9, 2007, Judge Michael Sauer again presided in judgment over Sutherland's misadventures. Although Sutherland was not in the courtroom, his lawyer Blair Berk represented him and read his statement into the record: "I am very disappointed in myself for poor judgment I exhibited recently, and I am deeply sorry for the disappointment and distress I have caused my family, friends, and co-workers on *24* and at 20th Century Fox." Although Sutherland pled no contest, Judge Sauer was not in a lenient frame of mind. He sentenced Sutherland to forty-eight days in jail—thirty days for the DUI and another eighteen days for the probation violation—as well as another five years of probation. The sentence also required compulsory enrollment in an eighteen-month alcohol-education program and weekly therapy sessions for a period of six months.

Sutherland was ordered to surrender no later than December 31, 2007, to begin serving his sentence. He was slated to serve time at the notorious L.A. County Twin Towers facility, known for its twenty-three hours of solitary confinement a day, albeit in brightly lit cells. An arrangement was worked out that would allow him to serve out his time in several blocks so that *24*'s shooting schedule would not be disrupted.

All plans changed on November 5, 2007, when the Writers Guild of America officially went on strike, forcing the shutdown of production on television shows and films involving its members. The seventh season of *24* had already started shooting; eight episodes, a third of the season, had been completed, and a debut date for Season Seven had been announced for January 13, 2008. Fox executives and the *24* team had to quickly decide what to do. They tried to make their decision based on what the fans of the show would expect rather than what worked for them in terms of convenience or expense. The final decision was announced by the

Fox scheduling boss, Preston Blackman, after it became clear that the strike would be a long and divisive one: "The seventh season of *24* will be postponed immediately to ensure that the season can air uninterrupted, in its entirety." Blackman later commented that it was "not a decision anyone wanted to make, but it [was] one based on how we feel the fans expect us to react to this situation. The fans have shown us that they love following the season from start to finish. To begin airing under the present circumstances [would] allow us to begin, but who knows when we [would] ever get to the end."

The suspension of the series led Sutherland to report to jail immediately so he could get his sentence over with and put the experience behind him. His lawyer had negotiated a change of location; he would serve his time at Glendale City Jail, where he reported for jail two days earlier than was required. Glendale Police Chief Randy Adams made it clear that Sutherland would not be treated any different from any other prisoner and that his celebrity meant nothing in his jail: "He can check that at the door on his way in."

Sutherland was met at the Glendale City Jail by Officer John Balian, who led him through the check-in. He was issued a regulation orange jumpsuit and was told he would not be allowed to smoke his beloved Camels while inside. Sutherland was given a laundry detail; for over a month and a half, he filled all of his work hours folding pillow cases and doing laundry. Officer Balian later told reporters that Sutherland was a model prisoner; he was cooperative, worked hard, and never griped about anything.

When reflecting on his jail term, Sutherland puts it in perspective, meaning in the past where it belongs. "Everyone imagines what the experience would be like and how you would handle it," he says. "I had this idea that I would work out and read books and then work out some more, like Denzel Washington in *The Hurricane*, but when

I tried to do a couple of push-ups I had a toilet beside my head on one side, and my bunk beside my head on the other side. So I just gave up and went back to bed." And while he was allowed two visits a day with people from a list he had provided, he had few visitors outside of his lawyer. "I just wanted to get this done with. I had it coming and I wanted to get it over with."

How did going without his Camels and his J&B scotch for forty-eight straight days sit with him? "I was not a big every-day kind of drinker, so that didn't bother me too much, and it was good to know that I could give up the cigarettes for that length of time. Maybe one day I will quit for good."

But for all the good-natured ribbing Sutherland aimed at himself about the experience, there were things about his time in jail that were not pleasant in the least: "Originally they told me that I was going to get a cell to myself. But when I got there it turned out that I had a cellmate for the first couple of weeks. Then he was released, but it wasn't long before he was right back in again." And the conditions inside the jail were not something he could even have remotely imagined. "In there," he explains, "I was locked up in a small room with the lights on all the time. You could not even cover your head with a blanket or cover the light with something; there were cameras in every cell."

"I can find some humor it looking back on it—you have to," continues Sutherland. "But there is nothing funny about the situation, really. Eighteen thousand people a year die in this country because of drunk driving; this is not funny by any means. But my personal experience in jail—it's like when you read a travel brochure and then when you get there the place is nothing like it seemed in the brochure. I can tell you, jail is exactly what you think it is going to be. It is exactly as advertised."

In another incident where Sutherland realized that jailhouse clichés were based on reality, he recalls: "I was in the shower, and I actually did drop the soap. I looked around and in my head I was yelling, 'You dropped the soap!' I decided that soap was overrated anyway and just left it there."

Sutherland was housed with dangerous L.A. gang members, many of them fans of Jack Bauer. "One day as I was cleaning up the trays after lunch and as I was heading back to the cell, one of the gang guys started flashing his gang signs at me, telling me who he was and what crew he was with," he says. "I didn't know what to do so I just gave him a big double thumbs-up. He found it pretty amusing."

Kiefer was not allowed outside at all during the time he was incarcerated. "We were allowed to watch television for a couple hours a day," he says. "But the guards decided what you watched, so we ended up watching many, many episodes of *Cops*."

* * * *

During the his son's arrest, trial, and incarceration, Donald Sutherland was constantly questioned about the incident and about Kiefer's behavior. On one occasion, the senior Sutherland told a reporter, "I applaud Kiefer's perfect behavior in the aftermath of his arrest. My son has conducted himself honorably, unlike a number of people during this whole situation. I will not name them but they know who they are." As his ire built, Donald added, "You don't want to get me going on this. All I can tell you is this, that Kiefer is the most honorable, responsible, decent man I know, and I love him with a passion. He behaved in a way that was so pure and perfect and respectful. There are other elements in our community that were less so, but he was perfect."

And Donald Sutherland's devotion continued throughout his son's imprisonment. Donald wrote Kiefer letters every other day while he was in prison and spoke to his son on the phone as often as he could. "Jail was very tough for him," says the father. "He had forty-eight days inside, twenty-three hours a day in solitary, and it was very, very cold. There were no windows. He had no community. I made a deposit at the prison so he could call out. We were given fourteen minutes for every call. When he would call, I often wasn't prepared, and when I got to speak to him I didn't get to say all the things I wanted to say."

Kiefer Sutherland spent his forty-first birthday, Christmas, and New Years Day in jail and was released on Monday, January 21, 2008. Because of the flock of reporters in wait at the front entrance, he was allowed to be picked up quietly at the rear of the building. That was the only concession to his celebrity that he was extended or that he even asked for.

On January 24, he met up with his dad in Santa Monica at one of their favorite restaurants for their reunion dinner. The two men hugged quite hard and long and were both clearly happy to see each other. Donald, ever the pragmatist, concludes the matter simply: "He made a mistake, a stupid mistake. But he took his punishment and now will go forward having learned from the whole thing. Did I like seeing my son going to jail? Not at all; it was difficult. So I hope I never have to see that again."

* * * *

His conviction caused some collateral damage that Kiefer Sutherland had not anticipated. After he completed his jail term, the organization Mothers Against Drunk Driving (MADD) vociferously protested against the notion of a four-time convicted drunk driver being the spokesperson and role model for a car company. Two seasons earlier, Fox and the Ford Motor Company had signed a multi-million-dollar sponsorship arrangement that made Ford the major sponsor of *24*. Sutherland acted as a voice-over spokesperson for the Ford Motor Company Canada commercials, and his raspy yet alluring voice had soon become recognizable as the voice of Ford on TV screens across North America.

MADD's official statement included references to the blatant irresponsibility of Sutherland's actions when he could easily afford a limousine or a driver to transport him when drunk. The group objected to the negative mixed message Sutherland embodied as Ford's spokesperson. The megacorporation took the complaint seriously and talked to Sutherland about it, but in the end Ford backed its boy. Sutherland can still be heard pitching the Ford Fusion Hybrid.

To his credit, in May 2008, Sutherland appeared in a stark full-page anti-drunk-driving ad in the *New York Times* for the American Beverage Institute. The ad featured Sutherland's police mug shot, as well as that of rock band Green Day's Billie Joe Armstrong, who also was arrested for DUI. The ad praises new technology that would prevent a drunk from even being able to start a car as well as new advances in Breathalyzer technology.

* * * *

After his release from jail in February 2008, Sutherland began dating Siobhan Bonnouvrier, the style director for Allure magazine, whom he had first met late in 2007. Many of her friends openly commented that jail was the best thing that had ever happened to the actor. It scared him straight. Events would soon prove that to not be true entirely, but being in jail had undoubtedly left a mark on Sutherland.

22

CHASTENED?

"What did I learn from going to jail? Don't go back!"

–Kiefer Sutherland

If the time Sutherland spent in jail tempered his behavior, the effects were not immediately obvious.

For his forty-second birthday, in December 2008, Sutherland's pals threw him a party at Ye Rustic Inn, a favorite bar of Sutherland's. Part of the festivities were to involve a sexy blonde stripper. After the booze had been flowing for quite some time, the lights dimmed and the blues music pumped up. The stripper slinked in, nearly naked save for a leopard-print teddy. Someone pulled up a chair for Sutherland and the stripper danced around him seductively, then began a lap dance, which he appeared to enjoy wholeheartedly. Then, instead of flinging off the G-string, the dancer tore off a blonde wig, revealing a semi-trans-gendered "she-male." Sutherland was enraged at first and violently shoved the stripper off his lap while his friends laughed hysterically. Sutherland took a few long moments to regain his composure, then spoke to the stripper, apparently apologizing. He then demanded explanations from those around him, his embarrassment that he hadn't detected the sex of his birthday present clear to all.

****

Every year at Oscar time, there are a few after-parties that have become almost as legendary as the Oscars themselves. *Vanity Fair* hosts a big affair, and for many years Sir Elton John has thrown an Oscar bash that both nominees and other famous people cram into after each ceremony. Sutherland attended Sir Elton's party on February 23, 2009, where he made an unusual spectacle of himself. While Sutherland is often a lovable drunk who wants to make people laugh, on this night he had an obnoxious edge, a vulgarity that got darker the more J&B he drank. "It was kind of embarrassing for him," a Hollywood publicist who was at the party says. "He was really sweating badly. His face was red, and whenever I saw him, he literally had a Scotch in each hand. He would swear at everyone who passed by him. It was crazy. One guy just walked up to the bar to ask for a drink. Kiefer was talking to the bartender, and he then turned to the guy and said, 'What the fuck are you looking at? Mind your own fucking business, asshole.' The poor guy frowned and then went right ahead and asked for the drinks he was there to get."

Then Sutherland and former Guns N' Roses guitarist Slash got into an expletive-riddled shouting match. It was hard to tell if it was good natured or not, especially because when the two attended a poolside party at The Mirage in Las Vegas several months later, they got along without incident. The publicist recalls, "Sutherland would call Slash something vulgar, like 'You fucking animal.' Then Slash would holler back, 'You fucking pussy, come over here and call me that.' " Sutherland was seen leaving the party at a relatively early hour, bumping into people and slurring his words. Before he left, he made sure he directed one more vulgarity towards Slash, while giving him the finger, and then he went out into the night.

* * * *

In early May 2009, Sutherland was in New York, where he had been staying for a variety of reasons. The eighth season of *24* was set in New York, and his new lady love Siobhan Bonnouvrier lived there as well. Also, his daughter Sarah Jude attends college in the city. On the evening of May 4, Sutherland was scheduled to attend a gala event at the Met Costume Institute Gala. Earlier in the day, he had been in the Rose Bar of the Gramercy Park Hotel, where observers say he had been knocking back drinks for a while and was running around wearing a giant feather boa and acting crazy. But later, when he arrived at the Met red carpet event, he was all smiles and was chatting amiably with people.

An astonishing event occurred when Sutherland later attended an after-party at the trendy Soho nightspot, SubMercer. At the club, Sutherland appeared drunk but calm. While he was chatting with his friend Brooke Shields, another friend of hers, Jack McCollough, a young designer for Proenza Schouler, headed toward them. According to McCollough, when he interrupted their conversation, an inebriated Sutherland took exception to the intrusion and insisted that McCollough apologize. "He was drunk and would not back down," says McCollough. "He pulled this stupid wrestling move on me like a teenager and then slammed his head into my face." Other guests nearby, including Mary-Kate Olsen and Kirsten Dunst, looked on in stunned amazement. When it was all over, Jack McCollough had a bloody injured nose.

A witness told the NYPD a different story, saying that in fact McCollough had barged over to Sutherland and Shields and had bumped into Shields, causing her to stumble. Sutherland grabbed Shields so she wouldn't fall to the ground, then demanded that McCollough apologize. When he wouldn't, Sutherland, as he had done many times before, acted with his booze-clouded impetuousness to teach McCullough a lesson.

The next day the media had a ball with the story. Reports had McCollough with everything from a small cut on his face to a broken nose. Pictures of him taken then next day showed that the damage was somewhere in between: he looked like he had been head-butted in the face. A spokesperson for Brooke Shields issued a statement saying, "Nothing happened to her. Jack did nothing inappropriate. It is not clear what caused Kiefer to do what he did." The representative clearly stated that McCollough, who designs clothes for Shields, "did absolutely nothing to her."

On hearing that there would be a police investigation, the *New York Daily News* headed to the address of Sutherland's girlfriend, Siobhan Bonnouvrier, to get the story. Sutherland answered the door but refused to comment. Sutherland's New York lawyer, Michael Miller, issued a statement saying, "We are troubled by the unauthorized and self-serving information regarding Kiefer Sutherland and the events of last Monday evening. We are confident, however, that the investigation done by the Manhattan district attorney and the NYPD will confirm that Kiefer Sutherland was neither the instigator nor a wrongdoer in the incident."

The district attorney nevertheless charged Sutherland with third-degree assault. Depending on the circumstances, this misdemeanor carries a penalty that ranges from a $1,000 fine to a year in jail.

Brooke Shields's lawyer, Gerald Lefcourt, issued a statement on behalf of his client that said simply, "Both Jack and Kiefer are friends of Ms. Shields, and she regrets this unfortunate situation."

On May 7, 2009, at 4:00 p.m., Sutherland, accompanied by his L.A. lawyer, surrendered to prosecutors at the Fourth Precinct in New York City. He was issued a desk-appearance ticket, was photographed and fingerprinted, then was left with his lawyer to make his way through the throng of reporters to an awaiting black Lincoln Town Car outside at the curb.

Sutherland then issued his first statement about the matter: "I am sorry about what happened that night and sincerely regret that Mr. McCollough was injured." This statement was not just spin; Sutherland has often said that every time he loses control and gets into a physical altercation where he is responsible for hurting someone, he always feels truly awful about it. When McCollough heard Sutherland's statement, he issued one of his own: "I appreciate Mr. Sutherland's statement, and I wish him well."

That night, Sutherland was in one of his favorite New York watering holes, a bar called Libation. A friend who was with him that evening says, "Kiefer just likes to have a good time when he can; he wasn't thinking, 'Oh, I've just been arrested after a drunken fight. I better be careful.' He doesn't think like that; he doesn't live like that. He had a couple of days in New York before heading back to L.A., and he was going to have a good time."

And while the evening at Libation produced no brawls or tree tackling, Sutherland did get plastered. His companion for the evening remembers, "Kiefer just wants to get to the happy, giddy place fast. He wants to get to the happy, goofy Kiefer quickly and leave Jack Bauer behind. He knocked back seven whiskeys and Cokes in the time it took me to go through one and a half. And it just went on from there."

A couple of days later Sutherland returned to Los Angeles, where he was to join up with the *24* team for a special advance screening of the final episode of Season Seven. Outside the theater, Sutherland was greeted with hugs and warm wishes from everyone, as though *he* had survived a head-butting incident and was making a triumphant return. It is a testament to how fondly he is thought of by his team. One of the biggest hugs Sutherland got was from fellow veteran actor Jon Voight, no stranger to public controversy himself, both through his own exploits and those of his daughter, Angelina Jolie. "How many times was Humphrey Bogart found sleeping off a drunk in a stranger's back yard?" says Voight. "Errol Flynn almost drank this town dry in his day. What Kiefer gets involved in is minor league stuff by comparison; it's just that now we have this insatiable voyeuristic need to always be watching people, not just in their public moments but in their private moments as well. We are all out here supporting Kiefer and our show because we all know Kiefer the man, and Kiefer the man is deserving of our love and respect."

Sutherland was clearly moved by the outpouring of affection he was receiving and said, "Well, on so many different levels, it's just like a big family."

* * * *

While the head-butting incident was being investigated by the NYPD, authorities in Los Angeles were checking into the possibility that the New York incident constituted a probation violation under California law. If it did, Sutherland could be sent back to jail. This would cause serious professional problems for him. On April 20, Sutherland had begun work in New York on a new Joel Schumacher film, entitled *Twelve*. Schumacher said that he would certainly stick by his friend in his time of trouble, but should Sutherland's situation compromise the film in any way then he would be forced to drop him from the film and re-cast the part.

Luckily, none of that ever became necessary. On July 21, the New York City district attorney's office announced that all charges against Sutherland stemming from this incident were being dropped. "This case does not even remotely qualify as criminal conduct," said the D.A. Los Angeles agreed, and all considered the matter closed.

The next day, on July 22, a clearly relieved Sutherland had a romantic picnic with his girlfriend Siobhan Bonnouvrier in Hudson River Park, near 12th Street. For several months Sutherland and she had been seen enjoying each other's company at various public places, including at a Beverly Hills fundraising dinner for Barack Obama, playing in the waves in Malibu, and strolling the streets of New York City hand-in-hand.

Friends of Bonnouvrier were saying publicly that she had a terrific effect on Sutherland and that they have seen changes in his behavior since he had been with her. A friend of Bonnouvrier's commented, "Even when they have little fights and squabbles about plans or such, Kiefer always backs down. Siobhan doesn't treat him like a star at all. He has a real respect for her, not just because he does, but because she demands it." Several people close to her also said that the couple was contemplating marriage.

Bonnouvrier was reported to be in love with Sutherland, but her solidity and experience with her own previous marriage make it unlikely that she would tolerate Sutherland's crazy and erratic behavior. As her friend put it, "Siobhan has told Kiefer that if they are to grow and build something serious, then he has to get control of his drinking and partying. And you can see it in his behavior—he is trying, or at least giving the impression that he is trying. He behaves himself when they are together, out for evenings or dinners. It's only when he's alone or with his guy friends that he acts like a drunken idiot. Never with Siobhan; she won't put up with it."

She apparently didn't, for by the end of summer, the couple had broken up.

In May 2009, as *24* moved on from a tumultuous Season Seven and began shooting Season Eight, there were mixed messages in the wind. Critically, the seventh season had earned positive reviews. Many, from *Variety* to the *New York Times,* opined that starting with *24: Redemption,* the series had regained some of its passion and velocity. But while the *24* team was feeling good about their accomplishments, the Fox brass was thinking of ending the run after Season Eight, when its current contract was due to expire. Fox executive Kevin Reilly came out and said, "It's our last contractual season of *24*. There are a lot of moving parts, so we are not sure what is happening after that. It's going to come down to a business decision. It is not an inexpensive show to make, and we want to make sure we finish strong. This is not a show we want to prop up; we just haven't made any decisions on it yet."

The writing staff of *24* was instructed to prepare scripts with alternative ending, so that in the case of a decision to end the series, an easy out could be effected at any time.

Sutherland's view of this is stark: "All of us, from the actors to the writers, understood from day one that individually, no one is the heartbeat of the show. If you look at the major characters that have been killed off during the run, you know that anyone can be killed off, and the show will get better without you. The real star of *24* has always been the concept." When asked about the prospect of having Jack Bauer killed off, however, Sutherland smiles: "When I go, I'll be going kicking and screaming."

The cast and crew that headed into Season Eight had seen highs and lows; they had been the trailblazers, and they had taken critical beatings. When *24* began, it was a bold try at something new and unique on television. As Season Eight dawned, many of the show's original people had left. Sutherland, a network TV novice at the beginning, was now a veteran TV superstar.

The studio, 20th Century Fox, had enjoyed milking its billion-dollar cash cow with *24* but was now actively contemplating its end. "The Hollywood landscape is different now," says Sutherland. "What shows like *The X-Files* and *Sex and the City* have shown is that there is a new direction to take a concept once its original TV-series has run itself through. There is only so much you can do to Jack [Bauer] before you lose realism. I think a movie would be a good way to end this story . . . I want it to be the most spectacular go-out-with-a-blaze-of-glory kind of thing. We will have this one opportunity to pull it all together." With his legal worries resolved, Sutherland was able to concentrate on the series and returned as an executive producer when shooting began on May 27, 2009.

On September 10, 2009, the Toronto International Film Festival kicked off, and there was a considerable Sutherland presence. One of the films being shown was *Cairo Time*, a film for which Sutherland's sister, Rachel, served as production manager. Another film that made its debut was *High Life*, which co-starred Kiefer's half brother, Rossif Sutherland. Rossif reveals that Kiefer still doesn't entirely believe in his own success: "It's amazing. I think even he is shocked. He has always really worked hard, though. He plays hard, too, as has been well publicized, but he also works really hard. I know a bit about that because I did a a regular stint on a series myself for awhile [he appeared on *ER* for eleven episodes in its tenth season]. I know what a grind it is, and he has been doing it for eight years."

One of the staples of the Toronto International Film Festival each year is the annual Canadian Film Centre barbecue. The Canadian Film Centre was founded twenty years ago by the Canadian-born, Oscar-winning director Norman Jewison, in North York. Also on the site is the Norman Jewison Director's School, which uses industry professionals as instructors and has had the likes of Clint Eastwood and Martin Scorsese drop by to show films and teach classes.

At his 2009 barbecue, Jewison took to the podium to announce that his friend Kiefer Sutherland would be joining him at the Canadian Film Centre to head up a new initiative: Sutherland was being named chairman of the CFC Actors Conservatory. After Jewison announced him, a dapper Sutherland came to the microphone and said, "I am honored to contribute to Norman Jewison's legacy by offering the CFC my passion for storytelling, for Canada, and its talent. The Actors Conservatory will have significant influence on the professional and creative lives of the actors attending and on our industry."

"I will give as much of my time as I can," said Sutherland. "The program will be open to eight or ten promising actors, and it will not exactly be a training course for learning how to act. This place is the Canadian Centre for Advanced Film Studies, as it was originally called, so what we are going to try to do is realistically guide them to a career. We will show them the reality of life as an actor."

Slawko Klymkiw, the executive director of the Canadian Film Centre, commented on Sutherland's appointment: "Kiefer Sutherland is very supportive toward his fellow Canadian actors. We are lucky to have him because he is going to be as hands-on as he can be. Not only that, he will be able to persuade other successful actors to join us as well."

Sutherland left Toronto without incident—no dancing on tables, no tackling trees—and headed back to Los Angeles for the Emmy Awards ceremonies on September 20. He was again nominated as best actor in a miniseries for his Jack Bauer portrayal, this time for *24: Redemption*. Irish actor Brendan Gleeson was also nominated in the same category for his brilliant portrayal of Winston Churchill in the film *Into the Storm*. When someone wished him luck at the Emmys, he laughed, "Are you kiddin' me? I'm up against Jack Bauer, aren't I?" But it was Gleeson who won the Emmy.

After the Emmy ceremonies ended, Sutherland headed straight for the Fox after-party at the nearby nightspot Cicada. He was the first to arrive. Although the staff was still setting up, he was allowed in. He headed straight to the bar, where he put on his sunglasses, which he hadn't worn outside, and ordered a J&B scotch and Coke. When the party reached full swing, Sutherland sat at a table with some Fox executives and had a few more drinks with them. Afterwards he left, alone.

* * * *

Professionally, Sutherland is now at something of a crossroads. His next big-screen appearance will be in a film called *Trust*, a Cold War drama. But where Sutherland as Jack Bauer is headed is still up in the air. There will be a feature-film version of *24*, but the studio's firm directive is to evaluate Season Eight before making any decision about the show's future. For his part, Sutherland plans on moving to New York City once Jack Bauer is out of his system. "I love it in New York; the people have a sexiness about them there that is quite extraordinary," he says. "Everyone is so full of purpose there; no one is just fucking around."

* * * *

When he leaves *24* and Jack Bauer behind, though, Sutherland will have imparted a legacy to television, an iconic role he made his own. It was as if Sutherland's whole being went into Jack Bauer, as if his whole career up until then was in preparation for this role. From his own personal experience, he knew intimately the emotional baggage the character carried. Sutherland had learned how to be a tough guy from the real-life tough guys he met on the rodeo circuit. He knew pain and challenge, both physical and emotional. He knew struggle, and how to keep busy no matter what. He knew that to stop would be to admit failure and die. That right there is the essence of Jack Bauer. And it is also the essence of Kiefer Sutherland.